D1217136

Elijah P. Lovejoy, Abolitionist Editor

University of Illinois Press

Urbana, 1961

ELIJAH P. LOVEJOY,

Abolitionist Editor

by Merton L. Dillon

 Library of Congress Catalog Card No. 61-62765.

For my mother and father

Preface

The antislavery movement in the United States gained great impetus in the 1830's as the abolitionists inaugurated their crusade for immediate emancipation. Their purpose was two-fold: they would attempt to convince all Americans, slaveholders and nonslaveholders alike, that slavery was a sin; at the same time, they would try to persuade them that the Negro, when he had been properly prepared for freedom, should be granted the same rights other citizens enjoyed. In short, the abolitionists envisioned themselves as carrying out a vast moral reform whose purpose was to revolutionize race relations in America. Their efforts to carry out that reform produced violent reaction in both North and South. In neither section did a majority agree with either of the abolitionists' chief contentions. They were not able within their own lifetimes to persuade Americans to accept their ideas and to implement them by effective social action. Their view of racial equality, especially, met with determined resistance. Indeed, it has not yet been proved that their ideas have ever been accepted with even approximate unanimity.

From that point of view, then, the abolitionist crusade must be considered a failure; for although the slaves were eventually freed, they were freed by the force of Union arms. This does not mean that the antislavery agitation contributed nothing to the destruction of slavery —without such men as Elijah Parish Lovejoy, Theodore Dwight Weld, James Gillespie Birney, and William Lloyd Garrison, there might not have been a Civil War and the consequent ending of slavery—but it does mean that history moved in paths other than those the abolitionists had expected. Emancipation did not result from the moral reformation of the slaveholders nor was emancipation accompanied either by contrition for past sins or by a determination to grant the freedmen equal political, social, and economic rights. Seen in that light, the struggles and the sacrifices of the abolitionists—even those of the Civil War armies themselves—are endowed with the added poignancy that accompanies all noble lost causes.

But whatever their success, men who engage in such titanic struggles inevitably command our attention and imagination. For that reason, if for no other, the abolitionists, with their single-minded devotion to the destruction of slavery, have long occupied a special place in American history. No one among them more clearly personifies their principles and their struggles than Elijah P. Lovejoy, whose brief career carried him from a quiet life as a schoolmaster in Maine to a violent martyrdom in Illinois.

I hope that my account of Lovejoy's life will contribute to an understanding of the pre–Civil War reform movements in general and of abolitionism in particular. The thousands of American abolitionists were not shaped in a common mold, however, and I make no claim that Lovejoy typifies the entire breed. But neither was he *sui generis.* A close study of his life and thought, therefore, ought to help explain the influences that led a sizable number of men to become abolitionists and to endure the consequences of that action.

The manner of Lovejoy's death did much to alter the course of antislavery agitation in the United States. It was never again to be quite the same for his having lived and died. But his importance is not confined to his participation in the antislavery movement, significant though that was. His steadfastness as an abolitionist editor places him in the long and honorable tradition of the defenders of a free press. More than that, his struggle to maintain his own rights and the rights of all men marks him as a member of that distinguished company who have asserted—often against formidable opposition and not always with success—the right of the unfettered individual to act in accord with his principles and to resist pressures that would force him to conform to popular will.

Many men who took up the struggle against slavery suffered as a result. A mob led William Lloyd Garrison through the streets of Boston with a rope tied around his body; mobs assailed Theodore Dwight Weld innumerable times; a mob whipped Amos Dresser. But of all the abolitionists, only Lovejoy was murdered for his beliefs. That fact in itself presents a situation worth analyzing.

Why did opposition to antislavery doctrine become so extreme that a mob in the free state of Illinois was willing to kill Lovejoy rather than allow him to continue his activities? On the other hand, what elements in Lovejoy's character and intellectual background made him persist in a course unpopular enough to imperil his life? This study attempts to answer those questions, and by so doing to illuminate the mentality of at least one prominent abolitionist and to recover some aspects of a frontier society faced by a problem it did not have the moral resources to solve.

But an account of Lovejoy's career also suggests several other questions for which I have supplied no answers. First, what is the responsibility of good men when agitators threaten to overturn the existing order? Second, are there limits to the extent to which moral problems may be settled by peaceful means? Are there, in fact, problems which human reason and human capacity for adaptation simply cannot solve at all?

I wish to take this opportunity to acknowledge my gratitude to Professor Dwight L. Dumond, who first introduced me to a serious study of the abolitionists, and to Professor Betty L. Fladeland, who read the manuscript at an early stage and made helpful and encouraging suggestions. Before Mr. and Mrs. Kenneth L. Wickett made their collection of Lovejoy family papers generally available by giving them to the Southwest Collection of Texas Technological College, they furnished me unrestricted access to them, a favor enriched by their generous hospitality. I should like also to acknowledge the courteous assistance of the library staffs at the American Antiquarian Society, the Boston Public Library, the Chicago Historical Society, the Chicago Theological Seminary, Colby College, the Connecticut State Library, Illinois College, the Illinois State Historical Library, the Library of Congress, the Massachusetts Historical Society, the McCormick Theological Seminary, the Missouri Historical Library, the Missouri State Historical Society, the Presbyterian Historical Society, Texas Technological College, and the William L. Clements Library.

Contents

A New England Beginning

Chapter I

If the Massachusetts farmers who lived along the Worcester Turnpike were watching the road in the last days of May, 1827, they might have seen an unfamiliar young man heading wearily along the dusty highway toward the West. He was Elijah Parish Lovejoy from Maine—tired, homesick, and nearly penniless—attempting to walk from Boston to Illinois. His sense of his sacred duty to God and to man had persuaded him that he must move to the West, but exactly what his mission was and how he would fulfill it he did not know. "I would fain have hope for the future," he confided to his journal, "but shadows, clouds and darkness rest upon it."[1]

Massachusetts was strange land to him, and as he passed through the state, by unaccustomed farms and through unfamiliar village streets, he felt himself friendless and alone, an outcast wandering in a far country. In another ten years practically everyone in the North would have heard his name. His abiding sense of duty would have secured his lasting reputation as an uncompromising abolitionist editor, the nation's most famous defender of the freedom of the press, a martyr for its cause. But just now, Elijah Lovejoy possessed no evident claim to distinction. To those who chanced to meet him on his journey, he must have appeared no different from the rest of the thousands of young men who at that moment were moving from the Eastern states

. . . . .

[1] Journal of Elijah P. Lovejoy, Elijah Parish Lovejoy Collection (Colby College Library, Waterville, Maine).

in pursuit of the dream that time and the West would bring them both fortune and the esteem of men.

And yet he was different from most, for as a classically educated descendant of an old Puritan family, he represented the rural elite class that had once dominated New England. In other days such a youth might easily have achieved distinction at home. But not any longer. City men—bankers, lawyers, manufacturers—were wresting leadership from the old Puritans of the villages and countryside. This youth on the Worcester Turnpike was leaving New England because its acquisitive society seemed to offer no place for such a man as he. Family tradition and training had not fitted him for life in an America now entering into the age of enterprise. He supposed, quite mistakenly, that the West would be different. There, he hoped, in some new settlement where leadership was still unformed he could make himself powerful and admired.

Elijah Lovejoy, eldest child of the Reverend Daniel and Elizabeth Lovejoy, was born November 9, 1802, near Albion, Maine, on the frontier farm his grandfather had begun to clear from the wilderness only a few years earlier. There in the small frame house overlooking the quiet waters of Lovejoy Pond, the seven Lovejoy children grew up in an atmosphere of stern Puritan morality and of sincere, though somewhat erratic, piety. The existence of absolute right and absolute wrong was a conviction the Lovejoy household accepted without question. From their infancy the children were taught to revere the Bible, to do their duty, and to suspect the pleasures and the standards that much of the world calls good. "The glitter of this world is captivating and a competency of its good things very desirable," Daniel Lovejoy once told his eldest son; "but our days are as grass," he added. "An unknown and endless eternity is just before us." A consideration so solemn led the Lovejoy children to scrutinize their minds and hearts constantly for evidence of their own fitness for eternity. It inclined them, too, toward critical examination of the society in which they lived.[2]

. . . . .

[2] Clarence Earle Lovejoy, *The Lovejoy Genealogy with Biographies and History, 1460-1930* (n.p., 1930), pp. 166-167; Joseph C. Lovejoy and Owen Lovejoy, *Memoir of the Rev. Elijah P. Lovejoy; Who Was Murdered in Defense of the Liberty of the Press, at Alton, Illinois, Nov. 7, 1837* (New York, 1838), pp. 13-17; Daniel Love-

Elizabeth Lovejoy, the mother, also was unusually devout. Indeed, the few of her letters that survive express a religious fervor far beyond the degree convention demanded of the professing Christian. Her religious views did not proceed altogether from undisciplined piety. She had thought much about spiritual matters, had in her youth discussed theological problems with clergymen who visited her father's home, and had studied serious works of systematic theology. She appears to have been at least as well informed on religious matters as her husband.[3]

The Reverend Daniel Lovejoy had tried with indifferent success to be both a farmer and a Congregational preacher. Deciding at the somewhat advanced age of nineteen to begin his formal education, he had left his father's farm to study at the academy in Byfield, Massachusetts, where he lived in the household of the Reverend Elijah Parish, the noted Congregational divine. The affection between the two had been great, and it was for Parish that Daniel Lovejoy named his first-born son. But the promise Elijah Parish had seen in the younger man was not to be realized. Daniel Lovejoy seems to have doubted his own convictions and ability, and a life of frontier hardship and disappointment only added to his debilitating lack of confidence. Fervently religious but short on learning and inclined to be quarrelsome, he was further handicapped by "an unnatural elevation and depression of spirits" that adversely affected his pulpit performance.[4] His unstable personality likewise produced its effect in the home, and as his daughter Sybil grew up, she too became "subject to great depression of spirits."[5]

In spite of these "depressed spirits" around him, Elijah Lovejoy—who was always called "Parish" by his family—spent a normal-enough childhood. Endowed with a strong, stocky body, this dark-haired, dark-eyed youth enjoyed all the usual boyhood sports, especially swimming in the lake conveniently located directly behind the house. Those activities, alternating with the wholesome labor of guiding the plow

joy to Lovejoy, October 20, 1823, Wickett-Wiswall Collection of Lovejoy Papers (Southwest Collection, Texas Technological College, Lubbock).

[3] Elizabeth Lovejoy, Autobiography, Wickett-Wiswall Collection.

[4] Lovejoy, *Memoir,* pp. 14-15.

[5] Elizabeth Lovejoy to Lovejoy, June 27, 1828, Lovejoy Collection.

and wielding the ax and the scythe, helped to spare him and his younger brothers, Daniel, Joseph, Owen, and John, from the most extreme forms of personality derangement. But even they, like their sister Sybil, possessed rather melancholy temperaments. Elijah, especially, suffered from a sharp sense of isolation at certain periods of his life.

Perhaps because he had himself failed to achieve his ambition to be a truly learned man, Daniel Lovejoy placed a particularly high value on education and encouraged his sons to become scholars. The demands for labor on the frontier farm and the family's lack of means limited the boys' opportunities for schooling, yet the children made full use of the resources available. Elizabeth Lovejoy taught Elijah to read the Bible when he was four years old and through the long Maine winters encouraged him to accomplish the precocious, if somewhat useless, feat of memorizing 150 of Isaac Watts' hymns. Before long the boy was reading the few theological books his father owned and borrowing others from the local library. As soon as he was old enough, he attended the public schools, and then, when time and money were available, the academies in the nearby towns of Monmouth and China. There he learned enough Latin and mathematics to qualify for entrance to Waterville College as a sophomore, just before his twenty-first birthday.[6]

In the fall of 1823 Elijah traveled from his father's farm for a dozen miles west, through the rolling wooded country of southern Maine to the town of Waterville on the Kennebec River. Waterville College, a Baptist-supported institution, was still a very new school in 1823, enrolling only a handful of students. Its professors were Baptist clergymen who, like the Lovejoys, believed in the moral order of the universe and in man's obligation to direct society along the paths they believed had been determined by the will of God. In that environment, Elijah, with his superior academic ability and his firm grounding in theology, experienced no difficulty in making a distinctly favorable impression. He was a model student, serious minded and introspective, with a taste for literature and a talent for writing effective, though overly romantic, poetry and prose. The faculty recog-

. . . . .

[6] Lovejoy, *Memoir,* pp. 17-19.

nized his potential and started him teaching in the college's preparatory division, persuading the Reverend Dr. Benjamin Tappan, a prominent Maine philanthropist, to supply the additional financial aid that made his continued attendance at the college possible.[7]

Even though Elijah was an unqualified success at Waterville (the college president thought him almost a genius), he was not a happy young man. Not then, or indeed ever, could he have been called carefree. One might, in fact, conclude that he belonged to that unhappy group upon whom the seriousness of life is impressed so early that they are never really young. Even as a youth the state of his soul cost him many hours of worry. From the time he was a child, his parents had impressed upon him the necessity for conversion, and yet he had reached manhood without experiencing that religious act. This fact pained him as much as it grieved his parents. "All that I know, and all that I feel," he wrote his father from college, "is, that religion is important, that I do not profess it, and that without it, I am miserable indeed."[8] At such moments his despair was unlimited, and he briefly considered self-destruction.[9] Although that mood soon passed, a feeling of isolation continued to haunt him. Partly, perhaps, it resulted from the alienation that sometimes awaits the man of simple origin who leaves the bounds of home to engage in the affairs of the world. But partly, too, it arose from the fact that he was a reformer as though by instinct, even when he did not consciously play that part. Much of the time his Puritan conscience, which parents and teachers had instilled in him from childhood, compelled him to disapprove of the society surrounding him. From the nature of things this brought him little satisfaction, for when society did not simply ignore him, it seemed to be rebelling against his disapproval. Consequently, he thought of himself as lonely, isolated, misunderstood. An element of prudishness and a sense of his own moral superiority contributed to his unhappiness. One vacation period he spent a few days with a rela-

. . . . .

[7] *Ibid.*, p. 19; Edwin C. Whittemore, *Colby College, 1820-1925, an Account of Its Beginnings, Progress and Service* (Waterville, Maine, 1927), pp. 38-39, 44; Waterville College Faculty Records, August 20, 1824, May 2, 1825 (Colby College Library).

[8] Lovejoy to Daniel Lovejoy, September 16, 1824, Wickett-Wiswall Collection.

[9] *Ibid.*

tive who kept a boarding house in the port town of Bath, Maine. A noisy, rowdy group patronized the place, or so it seemed to the inexperienced country boy. Only with the greatest difficulty could he continue his study of Virgil in that environment, he complained to his mother, constantly distracted as he was by the boarders' "shocking profanity and intemperance." He could not expect to obtain much "positive good" from such company, he moralized—except "to nauseate such licentiousness."[10]

When he was twenty-two years old and a student at Waterville, he seems to have been involved in a disappointing love affair, which must not have contributed to his sense of well being. "Of all that knew him few but judged him wrong," he wrote of himself at the age of twenty-five; "he was of silent and unsocial mood: Unloving and unloved he passed along: His chosen path with steadfast aim he trod, Nor asked nor wished applause, save only of his God."[11]

This lonely youth was graduated from Waterville College in September, 1826, at the head of his class. What was he to do now? Returning to the farm seemed out of the question, and though his parents and the faculty at Waterville would no doubt have rejoiced had he decided to enter the ministry, he had not yet felt the call to do so. Nonetheless, his training made him feel obliged to use his talents to improve the condition of humankind and, if possible, to persuade others to accept his own moral and religious views. About the most available career for a young man with Lovejoy's taste and education was that of schoolmaster; thus, during the first winter after his graduation, he taught in the academy at China, where a few years earlier he had been a student.[12] But schoolteaching in New England could not satisfy his demanding, though unformed, ambitions. His brilliant academic record had convinced both him and his professors that a more influential position awaited him. For a time he considered journeying to the South, probably to take a job as tutor in a plantation

. . . . .

[10] Lovejoy to Elizabeth Lovejoy, September 22, 1824, Wickett-Wiswall Collection.

[11] Daniel Lovejoy to Lovejoy, February 11, 1825, Lovejoy to Sybil Lovejoy, April 24, 1832, Wickett-Wiswall Collection; Lovejoy, *Memoir,* p. 30.

[12] *Program of the Commencement of Waterville College, Wednesday, August 30, 1826,* Lovejoy Collection; Lovejoy, *Memoir,* p. 27.

family; but warnings of the unhealthful climate in that region persuaded him to abandon the plan. His brother Daniel, younger than he by fourteen months, likewise chafed within Maine's narrow horizons, and in that same summer decided to leave the family homestead to seek his fortune in western New York.[13]

The most direct avenues to wordly success for a bright, ambitious New England provincial in 1827 led either by way of the city or the West, the route Daniel had taken. Elijah's pious teachers, still somewhat scornful of the growing cities, naturally advised him also to choose the West; for there, they believed, an earnest, highly moral young man could best fulfill his responsibility to a needful world. There he could best serve the cause of God.

Elijah knew they were right, that the need of the West was great and could not be denied. Many of the Eastern clergy, and laymen as well, were much concerned in those days about the problems created by the settlement of the new lands across the Appalachians. In the early years of the nineteenth century the West was growing so rapidly that even casual observers recognized that it would shortly be in political control of the nation. Many New Englanders felt distressed as they contemplated the rude culture of the region that was soon to rule them, for settlement seemed to be outrunning civilization. Apparently the much-cherished religion and morality of New England would shortly be submerged by an unschooled, uncouth, and unbelieving West. Naturally such an event would have far-reaching secular repercussions, but to the Protestant clergy—men like the Reverend Daniel Lovejoy and the faculty at Waterville—this meant far more than mere loss of personal influence: it meant that the spiritual reformation of the world, an essential part of the preparation for the millennium, would be incalculably delayed.[14]

To prevent such a catastrophe, the New England churches had formed missionary agencies and reform societies and had organized

. . . . .

[13] A. G. Jewett to Lovejoy, February 9, 1827, Daniel Lovejoy, Jr. to his parents, November 29, 1827, Wickett-Wiswall Collection.

[14] John R. Bodo, *The Protestant Clergy and Public Issues, 1812-1848* (Princeton, New Jersey, 1954), pp. 152-156; Ira V. Brown, "Watchers for the Second Coming: The Millenarian Tradition in America," *Mississippi Valley Historical Review*, XXXIX (December, 1952), 450-451.

them into a great campaign to convert and reform the West before the chance had passed forever. They worked with special urgency in the belief that they were directing—as one of them said—"the secret springs and silent movements that give origin to the national character and public manners. . . ." Their efforts, they believed, would determine the nation's character for centuries to come.[15]

But reform societies alone were not thought adequate to save the nation. Clergymen also encouraged pious New Englanders to move into the new communities as they were settled. There they would form a nucleus of virtue to leaven the unmoral Western masses.[16] Lovejoy, moral, religious, and anxious to be useful, was exactly the kind of man who could serve such a purpose, and his teachers knew it. When he expressed a certain lack of satisfaction with his career as schoolmaster at China Academy, they persuaded him to seek the broader vistas of the West. Only a little persuasion was needed, for he already had vague, romantic dreams of fame and power that he knew the changing society of New England could not satisfy, dreams that he convinced himself could best be realized in a new country.

Thus it was that in the spring of 1827, as soon as he had ended the term's work at China Academy, Elijah said goodbye to his family and took passage at Bath on a schooner bound for Boston, the gateway to a greater world. The trip proved unexpectedly difficult. Contrary winds prevented the ship from arriving in Boston until four days later, and Lovejoy was miserable most of the time—"Sick, sick, sick," he managed to scrawl in his journal. But as the vessel neared its destination, he felt better, and when Boston harbor came into view, he was prepared to enjoy the new experience to the fullest. He thought he had never before seen "so beautiful a prospect." On either side of the ship for as far as he could see rose the harbor islands "covered with green and studded with trees." In the background lay the city itself,

. . . . .

[15] Arthur E. Bestor, Jr., "Patent-Office Models of the Good Society: Some Relationships Between Social Reform and Westward Expansion," *American Historical Review,* LVIII (1952-53), 514-520; John Mason Peck to the Secretary, Massachusetts Baptist Missionary Society, September 12, 1825, *American Baptist Magazine,* n.s. V (1825), 376.

[16] Theron Baldwin to Asa Turner, February 19, 1830, Historical Letters (Illinois College Library, Jacksonville); *Home Missionary and American Pastor's Journal,* II (October, 1833), 118-119.

the religious hub of New England (of the world, some thought), with "its numerous spires and gorgeous temples" outlined against the summer sky. Boston, the scene of so many stirring events in the nation's history, aroused Lovejoy's most intense feelings of patriotism. As he watched the departure from the harbor of a frigate that had been captured from the British in the War of 1812, his mind filled with thoughts of "the glorious achievements" of his countrymen, and his "heart beat thick and proudly." It was all a memorable adventure for a young man who had never before been a hundred miles from home or seen cities grander than Bath and Waterville.[17]

Boston, though, was disappointing to him in practically every respect other than the sights it offered. After spending five days there without finding suitable employment that would provide money to support his travels, he decided to move on. He might have gone to almost any place in the West, but he chose Illinois, whose potentialities were just then becoming well known in New England. For several years, especially since the recent opening of the Erie Canal, settlers had been moving there from the East, and the clergy had recently given the new state special publicity by their extensive campaigns to send missionaries to that frontier. Thus Illinois became Lovejoy's goal as he set out on foot from Boston, carrying with him almost no money and having only the vaguest notion of what he would do when he reached his destination.

Even for a man of means, and in the best of circumstances, the trip would not have been easy. For Lovejoy, with little money to moderate the hardships, it proved a nearly impossible ordeal. The life of student and schoolmaster had not prepared him for the strain of long-distance walking. Consequently, as the days passed, he experienced a variety of ailments. He noted in his journal that he awoke in the mornings "full of aches and pains." Almost daily he suffered from "violent" headaches, and felt oppressed with "lassitude and weariness." One day he walked from nine o'clock in the morning until three in the afternoon "having eaten nothing save a cracker and a small piece of cheese." On such occasions he must have shared the sentiments of

. . . . .

[17] Journal of Elijah P. Lovejoy, Lovejoy Collection. All further details in the account of Lovejoy's walking trip are from this source, unless otherwise noted.

his wandering brother Daniel, who in his homesickness wrote his mother, "I miss your rye and indian bread most bitterly."[18] And Lovejoy met other difficulties. When he had become so tired that he could walk no farther, he paid a farmer forty cents to carry him ten miles in his wagon, only to discover later that the driver had cheated him by taking him only seven.

But at last in the middle of June, after what had seemed an eternity of walking, he reached New York City.[19] There he planned to stop for a while to rest and replenish his pocketbook. Somewhere in that bustling place, he supposed, he could find congenial employment to supply himself with the means to continue his travels in greater comfort. To his profound discouragement, however, New York proved nearly as disappointing in that regard as Boston. Some kind of literary work—perhaps a position with one of the several city newspapers—would have best suited his tastes, but the newspapers demonstrated no interest at all in his writing ability. At length the newly established *Saturday Evening Gazette* offered him a job, but not as a member of its editorial staff. The newspaper needed someone to peddle subscriptions, and though the pay was wretched, Lovejoy was too hungry to refuse.

After spending weeks walking from Boston to New York, he was employed to walk up and down the dusty streets in the summer heat, knocking on doors and buttonholing strangers in the interest of the *Gazette*. For nearly five weeks he did this from sunup to sundown, earning scarcely enough to buy two meals a day. All in all, it was a frustrating experience for an ambitious college graduate who had enjoyed at least some confidence in his ability to earn a living through the academic skills he had acquired.

He was getting nowhere, and Illinois seemed as far away as ever. The only possible source of help he could think of was the faculty of Waterville College, the men who only a few months earlier had expressed so much faith in his talents and been so sanguine about his future. In desperation he sent a letter to the Reverend Jeremiah Chaplin, president of the college, explaining his predicament. As Lovejoy expected, Chaplin felt a responsibility to help his former stu-

. . . . .

[18] Daniel Lovejoy to Elizabeth Lovejoy, November 29, 1827, Wickett-Wiswall Collection.

[19] Lovejoy to an unnamed person, fragment, [1827], Wickett-Wiswall Collection.

dent reach the West where he might serve the cause of Christianity and New England ideals. Chaplin soon dispatched the money Lovejoy so sorely needed. "May the God of the wretched reward him ten thousand fold," Lovejoy wrote in gratitude.

Now with cash in his pocket, Lovejoy escaped from the New York treadmill and headed once more for Illinois, this time by way of the Erie Canal. The rest of the trip was easier, although he was delayed for a time in western New York when he fell ill from a malarial fever that left him temporarily wasted in body and melancholy in spirit. But finally in the autumn of 1827 he ended his long journey at the home of John Tillson of Hillsboro, Montgomery County, in the prairie country of western Illinois. Tillson, a transplanted Yankee Presbyterian reformer who interested himself in all good causes, made a practice of befriending young immigrants while they were establishing themselves in the West. Lovejoy could feel a special kinship with this kindly man and his family, whose ideas and attitudes were so like those of the ministers and teachers he had known in Maine, and Tillson probably welcomed Lovejoy as an additional New Englander bearing intellectual equipment for the reformation of the West.[20]

In the congenial atmosphere of Tillson's spacious new home, the only brick house in the whole county, Lovejoy recuperated from the mental and physical ordeals of the summer. All was not success, however, for as soon as he recovered and began to look for a way to make a living, he discovered that the sparsely settled land of Illinois afforded little work of the kind he sought. Illinois was still frontier. As yet there was little need or even toleration for scholars or reformers or romantic, moody young men. There in that raw land, even as in New England, leadership appeared to go to speculators and merchants rather than to the carefully reared, classically educated men of Puritan conscience. But only a few miles away lay the thriving river town of St. Louis. St. Louis would not be like Waterville or Boston, he knew; still in this prosperous setting he supposed that he could easily find an opportunity to work for his own material welfare and also for the good of Christian society.

In those expectations he might well be disappointed, for, as he

. . . . .

[20] Daniel Lovejoy to Lovejoy, January 15, 1828, Lovejoy Collection; A. T. Strange, "John Tillson," *Journal of the Illinois State Historical Society*, XVII (1924-25), 719-721.

would shortly learn, the people of St. Louis were not likely to welcome the efforts of a New Englander to shape them into conformance with his own moral pattern. More than almost any other city in America, St. Louis typified the dynamic spirit of the rising West. By the spring of 1828 its population had reached nearly 5,000, with new settlers arriving daily, a large portion of them young men, each jostling for position in an economy and society where most lines of division remained fluid. The new arrivals represented every kind of background, every shade of opinion, and each was zealous to maintain his own independent views and to support his own ambitions. About the only opinion shared in common in that fiercely competitive environment was an antipathy for restraints. Lovejoy would find little sympathy among those ambitious, undisciplined Westerners for his restrictive moral principles and religious convictions.

Lovejoy would find himself, too, in a society far more secular than any he had ever known before. In New England his puritanical strictures and self-righteous criticisms, however much resented, would still be tolerated, even by those who refused to heed them, for they were the expression of an orthodox religious and moral tradition that had not yet been overthrown. St. Louis possessed no such tradition. Its churches, small and weak like all other Western institutions, had influenced only a minor part of the population. Indeed, many of its new settlers were aggressively hostile toward organized religion of any kind. No Congregational church existed in the area. Methodists and Baptists formed the city's largest Protestant groups, although a recently formed Presbyterian church had begun to prosper, especially among settlers from the Northern states. Far larger than any of these denominations was the Roman Catholic church. At the time Lovejoy arrived in St. Louis, most of the Roman Catholics were descendants of the old French inhabitants, whose religious views were rather lightly held. They were soon to be augmented, however, by an influx of Irish immigrants, who took their religion quite seriously and who challenged the growing Protestant influence in the region.[21]

. . . . .

[21] Rufus Babcock, *Forty Years of Pioneer Life; Memoir of John Mason Peck, Edited from His Journals and Correspondence* (Philadelphia, Pennsylvania, 1864), pp. 85-88; Timothy Flint, *Recollections of the Last Ten Years*, ed. C. Harley Grattan (New York, 1932), pp. 103, 109-113, 173-174.

All in all, it was an exhilarating atmosphere—and a dangerous one—that Lovejoy prepared to enter. St. Louis, located near the confluence of the Missouri, Mississippi, and Ohio rivers, served as a converging point for mid-America. It stood at the crossroads of the continent. Anchored at its narrow wharf lay the steamboats that had delivered cotton and sugar from the plantations of the South, flour and iron from the mills and factories of the East. Down the broad and sometimes savage rivers that led from the North and West moved the fur traders, rough and only half tamed, who brought a part of the wilderness with them whenever they returned to civilization. From out of the glowing vastness of the Southwest came nineteenth-century merchant adventurers, men who had traveled the long trail to the exotic Mexican outpost of Santa Fe. Geography had made St. Louis more cosmopolitan than most American cities. If there was a spot where the diverse strands of the American continent were bound together, this was it.

But precisely because St. Louis was diverse and innocent of the moral focus that characterized the New England villages Lovejoy had known, his restrictive ideals were not likely to find favor with a large part of the city's population. A people confronted by so many secular opportunities did not have time to take seriously pleas for reform and repentance; nor did they have patience with men who preached to them about social responsibilities. Nonetheless, in the fall of 1827 Lovejoy moved into the expanding economy and fevered society of St. Louis. The rough-and-tumble competition of the warehouse area; the rude traders who returned with their haul of furs from out in the wilderness, the smell of the Indian camps still strong upon them; the bawdy life of the river front—those things only disgusted the young Eastern scholar who had been so grossly offended by the "grog shops on the road" and the "drunkards staggering the streets" of his native Maine.[22]

All societies are perhaps afflicted by that kind of schism. On the one hand are those persons heedless of moral order, who stand always ready to escape from the trammels imposed by the past and, in their haste to profit and pleasure from the abundance of this world, return

. . . . .

[22] Journal of Elijah P. Lovejoy, Lovejoy Collection.

more or less unwittingly to a natural, unregulated existence. A pole apart from them is another, smaller group, whose members scrupulously labor to preserve the institutions, the ideas, and the values that have been transmitted to their generation from some other time or place. Western communities in America especially witnessed such a division, and few of them more dramatically than the cities of the central Mississippi River valley, where sometimes the division erupted into violence. There Elijah Lovejoy was to spend the few years that remained of his life, always a participant in the struggle between those forces, eventually dying in the midst of their dubious battle.

Reforming Politics

Chapter II

When Lovejoy had oriented himself to the situation in St. Louis, he experienced no difficulty making up his mind which portion of the society in his new home was superior and to which part he belonged. "Northerners," he early assured his parents, "constitute the most orderly, most intelligent, and most valuable part of the community." Their interests and their outlook were his as well. Because that was so, he could more easily establish himself prosperously and usefully among them.[1]

Since Missouri in 1828 had not yet established a system of public education, private schools, a type of institution Lovejoy already knew a good deal about, still flourished in the towns. So it was that he hit upon an acceptable way to earn his living. He decided to establish his own private classical high school in St. Louis. He would pattern it after the academies of the East and seek the patronage of the "most valuable part of the community."

Prospects appeared good that such an enterprise would make an ample living, and it might at the same time serve in a small way to strengthen New England culture in St. Louis. His family back in Maine, hoping the school would do precisely that, offered prayers that it might become the instrument for effecting a general moral and religious reformation in the city. Lovejoy was more modest in his expectations. A reformation he no doubt would have welcomed, for he

. . . . .

[1] Lovejoy to his parents, February 18, 1827, Lovejoy, *Memoir,* p. 33.

adhered to the moral code of the East and despised reckless living wherever he encountered it. But while the background and attitude of the reformer were already his, he had not yet consciously assumed the religious reformer's role. Although Lovejoy certainly hoped his project would be useful, the school he established in the spring of 1828 had a purpose hardly larger than its prospectus stated: to teach classical studies to the young men and women of St. Louis.[2]

Even this goal might have seemed too ambitious for that Western community, most of whose members had little respect for tradition or the dead hand of custom. Still the school prospered; and during the two years Lovejoy conducted it, he was able to send money home to his father and also to accumulate a little capital and a degree of prestige, remarkable in a city whose most conspicuous elements respected values other than those offered by a classical education.[3] But in spite of Lovejoy's material success, schoolteaching in St. Louis failed, as it had in Maine, to satisfy all his ambitions. The lure of fame, the desire for public influence, and an increasing zeal for reform soon led him to abandon the schoolroom forever.

In the summer of 1830, T. J. Miller, the publisher of the St. Louis *Times,* began to look for a new partner. Lovejoy welcomed the opportunity, for a journalistic career represented everything he most desired. It would give him the occasion he had long sought to employ his literary skill, it would satisfy his urge to express his opinions where they might be widely heard, and above all, it would provide him with a means to influence society. Back in Maine his mother appraised his new plans. He was now "associated with the wise and good," she wrote, and appeared "to be active in the great and glorious work of evangelizing the world. . . ."[4]

As quickly as possible, he sold his school, and in August, 1830, became senior partner in the firm of Lovejoy and Miller on Locust Street, publishers of the St. Louis *Times.*[5] The *Times,* a political newspaper, had been founded the year before by Miller and Jacob R. Stine

. . . . .

[2] Elizabeth Lovejoy to Lovejoy, June 27, 1828, Lovejoy Collection; *Missouri Republican,* March 4, 1828.

[3] *Missouri Republican,* December 30, 1828; Lovejoy to his parents, March 15, 1829, Wickett-Wiswall Collection.

[4] Elizabeth Lovejoy to Sybil Lovejoy, June 18, 1830, Wickett-Wiswall Collection.

[5] St. Louis *Times,* August 14, 1830.

to support Andrew Jackson's administration. The partners had soon disagreed, however, and the paper had not prospered. Indeed, it was on the point of failure when Stine sold out to Miller in January, 1830. When Stine left, the *Times* became critical of President Jackson. After Lovejoy bought into the firm, it openly espoused the cause of Henry Clay and his program of protective tariffs and internal improvements.[6]

The new editorial partners plunged at once into the roaring sea of political journalism. The early 1830's were particularly turbulent in both politics and journalism, a period when even obscure party factions supported their own newspapers and barred few holds in the struggle to gain advantage. It was a time when editors relied nearly as much on ridicule and studied insults to damage their rivals' cause as they did on reasoned arguments.

Lovejoy and Miller proved entirely capable of playing their part in this unsavory game, receiving little worse than they gave. When the St. Louis *Beacon,* a Jacksonian paper, referred slightingly to Lovejoy as the "ex-schoolmaster," and in a particularly sharp piece characterized him as a "little animal," the *Times* ridiculed the *Beacon*'s "whining" and termed the whole enterprise "ludicrous" and "despicable."[7] Later, the editor of the *Beacon,* affecting to believe the story of one of the *Times*'s journeyman printers who claimed he could not collect his wages, printed a solemn exposé of Lovejoy and Miller, portraying them as heartless exploiters of honest workingmen. The *Times,* of course, issued a denial quite as solemn, and the battle of words continued.[8] If the *Beacon* seemed especially peevish when Lovejoy and Miller were concerned, it was perhaps because the *Times* had earlier printed the startling remark that the *Beacon*'s editor was "a mere inflated bladder of—mephitick gas—and that is the opinion of more than '9 out of 10!!' "[9]

But such insults and charges were conventional and not to be taken very seriously, least of all by the men directly involved. Lovejoy and

. . . . .

[6] St. Louis *Beacon,* January 30, 1830; *Missouri Republican,* July 6, 1830; St. Louis *Times,* July 24, August 28, November 20, 1830.

[7] St. Louis *Beacon,* October 14, 1830, November 3, 1831; St. Louis *Times,* October 30, 1830.

[8] St. Louis *Beacon,* September 30, 1830; St. Louis *Times,* October 9, 1830.

[9] St. Louis *Times,* July 31, 1830.

Miller did not allow the space they devoted to these verbal pastimes to obscure their well-defined political position. The *Times* was a partisan newspaper designed to promote the candidacy of Henry Clay for the presidency of the United States. In 1830, however, Andrew Jackson held that office, and the editors of the *Times* made it clear that they approved neither of him, his party, nor his policies. "With an adulterer and murderer for our President, and fools and knaves for his advisors, if we survive, then shall I indeed believe that Providence intends to perpetuate our system," wrote Lovejoy shortly after Jackson's inauguration.[10]

The decade of the 1820's had seen great advances toward the political democratization of the country, with the extension of suffrage to increasing numbers of the people. Jackson was generally thought to have been elected by these new voters and to represent the views and aspirations of the common man. Though many considered this an entirely satisfactory situation, Lovejoy, like many of the Eastern clergy whose views he often mirrored, was far from enthusiastic. He was not pleased with the rapidly emerging democracy of his time, for it meant the creation of a new political majority which, at least for the moment, appeared to possess neither the intelligence nor the virtue rulers ought to have. This is, of course, another way of saying that the new electorate often did not vote the way New Englanders wanted it to.[11]

For similar reasons Lovejoy regretted the development of the type of blind party loyalty which held that a "Jacksonian" must support "Jacksonians" for office without regard for the qualifications of individual candidates. The *Times,* like other opponents of Jackson, advanced the contrasting position that only men of "influence, capacity, and dignity" merited election to public office—a barb clearly aimed at the Jacksonian party's implied rejection of the premise that training, knowledge, and demonstrated ability were requisite for the holding of office.[12] Nor was the *Times*'s position simply political opportunism. Men like Lovejoy held no political conviction more firmly than their belief that government must be built squarely on a moral and religious foundation, ...

[10] Lovejoy to his parents, March 15, 1829, Wickett-Wiswall Collection.

[11] Bodo, *Protestant Clergy,* p. 154; Sidney Earl Mead, *Nathaniel William Taylor, 1786-1858; a Connecticut Liberal* (Chicago, 1942), pp. 79-82.

[12] St. Louis *Times,* October 30, 1830; Stephen Pettis to Lovejoy, May 27, 1831, Lovejoy Collection.

which meant that both voters and officeholders must display the attributes of religion and morality. Such qualities they did not expect to find abundant in the natural man. Only in the able and the educated did they believe the qualifications necessary for civic responsibility were likely to exist.[13]

The basis for Jacksonian power did not satisfy Lovejoy and Miller, nor did they approve of Jackson's political policies. The editors favored a tariff to encourage manufacturing and internal improvements to stimulate the growth of the West. This, of course, formed the heart of Clay's American system, a program which the *Times* claimed would make the United States "feared and respected abroad, and independent, rich, happy, and contented at home." And Jackson's administration, as every one knew, had been hostile toward both the tariff and internal improvements. They did not approve, either, of Jackson's plans to remove the Indians of the Old Southwest across the Mississippi River, a policy they condemned as "both impolitic and unjust," a scheme of "iniquity and oppression."[14]

Lovejoy's anti-Jackson policy reached into state politics, with tragic results. In 1831 when Representative Stephen D. Pettis, a friend of Thomas Hart Benton and a supporter of Jackson, announced his intention to run for renomination to Congress, Lovejoy printed articles against him prepared by a writer who signed himself "Missouri." When Pettis demanded that Lovejoy disclose the identity of his detractor, Lovejoy at first delayed and then—according to Pettis—reported, falsely, that the author had left St. Louis. He was Thomas Biddle, director of the St. Louis branch of the Bank of the United States and a brother of Nicholas Biddle. Pettis wrote a sharp reply to Biddle, thereby precipitating a brawl with Biddle, Benton, and Pettis taking part. A few weeks later Pettis and Biddle fought a duel in which both men were mortally wounded.[15]

During the years Lovejoy edited the *Times,* almost the last remains of the nationalistic sentiment that had characterized the decade following the War of 1812 faded away. As a belligerent sectionalism displaced the nationalistic temper of an earlier day, Clay's American system,

. . . . .

[13] Bodo, *Protestant Clergy,* pp. 154-156; Lovejoy to his parents, March 15, 1829, Wickett-Wiswall Collection.

[14] St. Louis *Times,* October 9, August 28, September 18, 1830.

[15] Pettis to Lovejoy, May 27, 1831, Lovejoy Collection; William N. Chambers, *Old Bullion Benton, Senator from the Northwest* (Boston, 1956), pp. 177-178.

born of nationalism and designed to create a national economy, became a lost cause. The events of 1830 were likely to make any advocate of Clay's program conscious that the sectional differences that had developed within the United States imperiled nationalistic legislation, and perhaps the Union itself.

Lovejoy had always been aware that he was a New Englander and was proud of the distinctive culture of his section. But as a boy he had also exulted in a kind of romantic nationalism that knew no region. Now, however, as he saw the political policies he approved of assailed by Southern congressmen and the Union he loved threatened by Southern statesmen, his own regional self-awareness sharpened. In December, 1829, the legislature of South Carolina adopted John C. Calhoun's *Exposition and Protest,* reaffirming the doctrine of state sovereignty and the device of nullification to prevent the operation of national law within the state. A month later, Daniel Webster and Robert Hayne held their great debate over the nature of the federal Union, with Hayne, the Senator from South Carolina, expounding the doctrine of nullification on the floor of the United States Senate. Lovejoy, whose heart had beat "thick and proudly" with patriotism when he first viewed Boston, could only deplore the "South Carolina doctrine," which prevented the enactment of the American system and seemed to forecast the disintegration of the Union.[16]

Thus as early as 1830, Lovejoy, along with other proponents of the American system, developed hostility toward the aims and sentiments of Southern politicians. Later it would not be difficult for them to extend their hostility to include a critical examination of the South's peculiar social and economic institutions. More was involved in the growing Northern antipathy toward things Southern than simply moral considerations. Distrust of Southern political and economic programs had preceded and in some respects prepared the way for the dynamic antislavery campaign of the 1830's.

While Lovejoy's new interest in politics was leading him to oppose the administration of Jackson and the doctrines of Calhoun, he was also paying close attention to the ideas and programs of the Eastern reformers, enterprises still closer to his heart than was politics. Currently the reformers were engaged in a campaign to spread Eastern

. . . . .

[16] St. Louis *Times,* September 18, November 6, 1830.

morality and religion in the West with the greatest speed. They had organized the American Bible Society to spread the printed Gospel, the American Home Missionary Society to send preachers, the American Tract Society to supply easily read moral publications, the American Sunday School Union to form religious schools for the children, and various other specialized societies to combat the West's specific sins and vices. Lovejoy consistently sympathized with their efforts as a means of increasing the virtue of the electorate, but more especially as a means of promoting the kingdom of God.

He took an active part in some of the reform societies, attending their local meetings and going to hear reform lecturers when they happened to come as far west as St. Louis. He heard Lorenzo Dow, the Methodist missionary, and probably he met Theodore Dwight Weld (who was later to win fame as one of the greatest of the abolitionists) when he lectured in St. Louis on temperance and manual labor schools in 1832.[17] He heard Robert Owen, too, early in 1828, but Owen's antireligious and communitarian ideas seemed much too extreme to Lovejoy, whose views on most subjects were thoroughly conventional. Owen was a menace to society, Lovejoy thought, and he contributed an article to a St. Louis newspaper in which he said as much.[18]

Lovejoy interested himself in most of the public issues other religious reformers were interested in—he suggested the establishment of a lyceum in St. Louis to serve as a forum for their discussion—but the only reform society he actually joined during this stage of his career was the Missouri and Illinois Tract Society, an organization established to distribute pamphlets against such offenses as drinking, swearing, and Sabbath breaking. In 1831 he was elected its recording secretary.[19]

The most significant reform of all in the 1830's, however, was not one Lovejoy dabbled in—it was the antislavery movement. While Lovejoy was busying himself with political journalism in St. Louis, William Lloyd Garrison back in Boston had published the first issue of his

. . . . .

[17] *Ibid.*, August 21 and 28, 1830, March 5, April 16, 1831.

[18] *Missouri Republican,* March 25, 1828. Lovejoy's marked copy of this issue is in the Wickett-Wiswall Collection.

[19] Missouri and Illinois Tract Society, *Fourth Annual Report* (St. Louis, Missouri, 1831).

newspaper, the *Liberator,* on New Year's Day in 1831. Garrison, ready to abandon all halfway measures on the question of abolishing slavery, insisted that the slaves must be freed at once, irrespective of consequence. Garrison's imperious demand was not exactly new doctrine, yet the note of urgency in his message shook the whole country, North and South, in that unsettled time. Lovejoy, far away in St. Louis, probably read early issues of the *Liberator* since Garrison made a special point of sending them to editors in the slave states, but at the moment, Lovejoy showed little interest in abolition. His brother Joseph became one of the *Liberator*'s agents for Maine less than a year after the newspaper first appeared, and his mother soon counted herself a Garrisonian. Elijah, however, held back. In fact, he privately expressed his distaste for the doctrine of immediate emancipation.[20]

When Garrison's ideas reached him, he was somewhat interested in the work of the local branch of the American Colonization Society, a mildly antislavery organization which aimed to encourage masters to free their slaves voluntarily and to provide for the removal of free Negroes to Africa. But his main concern was still politics and general moral reform. Thus far, he had demonstrated no particular antipathy toward slavery or sympathy for the Negro; indeed, his newspaper continued to print advertisements offering slaves for sale, and he arranged to hire a Negro boy from a local slaveowner to work in his newspaper office.[21]

For a newspaper editor of his religious background, Lovejoy as yet had displayed remarkably little interest in that portion of the reform movement with which he was to be forever identified, the cause for which he was to give his life. Politics and the evils of blasphemy and hard drinking concerned him more in 1831 than did slavery. But a man with his Puritan conscience could not long ignore the insistent call of other kinds of reform. As the year 1831 came to an end, Lovejoy was about to undergo the momentous change in his life that would take him out of the backwaters of philanthropy and politics and launch him directly into the current of contemporary reform.

. . . . .

[20] Boston *Liberator,* October 1, 1831; Lovejoy to Elizabeth Lovejoy, April 1, 1833, Wickett-Wiswall Collection.

[21] St. Louis *Times,* July 9, 1831, September 4, 1830; William Wells Brown, *Narrative of William W. Brown, an American Slave* (London, 1849), pp. 26-29.

Conversion

Chapter III

From the day of his birth Elijah Lovejoy had lived in a religious atmosphere. In the home where he grew up at Albion and in the college he attended at Waterville, religion was as much taken for granted as the clear Maine air he breathed. Even after he moved to the faraway city of St. Louis, he remained intimately associated with the Protestant church and its clergy. Their influence was permanent upon him. His mother's prayer that he might be "preserved from the many temptations and vain allurements of this ensnaring but deceptive world" was not really necessary, even when he lived in so earth-bound a region as Missouri. He could never eradicate the indelible imprint left by the religious training of his youth.[1]

But for some reason that perhaps not even he could have explained, he had never formally joined a church or undergone the profound religious experience known as conversion, by which the penitent rejected sin and dedicated himself to the single-minded service of the kingdom of God. One need not take seriously Lovejoy's heightened image of himself as "the chief of sinners." Nonetheless, his youthful outlook, however moral, was decidedly worldly. He had longed more ardently for success than for salvation; he had sought fame with more diligence than he had exerted to cultivate piety. Sensuality bound him firmly to the earth. One evening on his trip from Maine he had met "3 or 4 buxom wenches . . . bare-footed and bare-legged" in a

[1] Elizabeth Lovejoy to Lovejoy, April 27, 1829, Wickett-Wiswall Collection.

tavern at Chesterfield, Massachusetts. He was not attracted to them, one supposes, merely by the fertile opportunity they doubtless provided for spiritual reformation. Only dogged conscience, he ruefully confessed, prevented him from tarrying overnight to "make their further acquaintance." As he prospered in St. Louis, he found he enjoyed the delights of good living almost too much. With the improvement in his finances he took lodging at the City Hotel, which provided superior accommodations, including a well-supplied table—Lovejoy's favorite delicacies were mallard and canvasback duck. This pleasure enjoyed by a young man did not necessarily suggest a nature confirmed in evil, of course, but it was hardly indicative, either, of a soul dedicated to the highest of purposes. His whole being inclined toward sin, he confessed, and he obstinately resisted all the efforts of those who labored to persuade him to devote himself to the cause of Christianity.[2]

Yet, however resistant he may have been, he had always remained faithful to religion in his fashion, constantly interesting himself in church enterprises and often flirting with reform. Thus in 1830 he had undertaken the editorship of the *Times,* firmly convinced that by so doing he promoted—as he phrased it—"the true principles of liberty and morality."[3] His ministerial friends certainly would have scoffed at that pretension, for to the Western clergy in the 1830's, who had chosen more direct reform methods, the editing of a political newspaper appeared to be a singularly oblique means for converting the world. Their procedure was both more personal and more dramatic. Holding revival meetings to bring new converts into their churches, they were then laboring to interest the new members in the great social questions of the day and to inspire them to work for the renovation of humanity through a complex structure of reform societies. Lovejoy was to remain not much longer on the periphery of their enterprises. His efforts to promote "liberty and morality" would presently be merged with the major reform movements of the era.

By 1830 a high wave of religious enthusiasm was sweeping across

. . . . .

[2] Lovejoy to his parents, January 24, February 22, 1832, Lovejoy, *Memoir,* pp. 39-41.

[3] "To the Patrons of the Times," St. Louis *Times,* February 18, 1832.

the United States. Although the revival affected all Protestant denominations to some extent, it was the liberal wing of the Presbyterian church that especially profited from it. The left-wing group in the church had rejected the Calvinistic doctrine of the utter sinfulness of man and the uselessness of "means" to effect conversion. Adopting the "new measures" popularized by the evangelist Charles G. Finney in western New York, the liberal Presbyterians succeeded in winning a host of converts through the use of such novel devices as protracted meetings, the "anxious seat," and small conferences for the instruction of "earnest inquirers." Though opposed by many more orthodox churchmen, Finney's methods proved remarkably effective, especially among people already religiously inclined. Many a young man of pious upbringing and earnest demeanor, who out of a kind of worldly pride had not yet joined a church, was overwhelmed by the "new measures" and found his attitude and the whole emphasis of his life altered as a result.

So it was with Lovejoy. In the spring of 1831 the great revival finally reached St. Louis. Lovejoy attended the protracted meetings held at the First Presbyterian Church in June, but though he hoped and prayed to be converted (as he told his parents), the meetings left him only "somewhat seriously impressed," and not a member of the group of eighteen converts reaped at that revival harvest. As he became absorbed once again in politics and the routine of newspaper work, his interest lapsed altogether.[4]

The next winter, however, the Reverend William S. Potts, pastor of the First Presbyterian Church, decided to call in the Reverend David Nelson of Palmyra, Missouri, to help him conduct a new series of special religious services. He could hardly have chosen a more effective colleague. Nelson, a flamboyant antislavery preacher, and revivalist who had mastered the use of extravagant language and vivid imagery, possessed rare ability to play upon the emotions of his audience. His was no ordinary determination. The agitated persistence that characterized each of his endeavors, whether in the work of evangelism or in controversy, left its mark wherever he chose to direct his powerful

. . . . .

[4] Charles Hempstead Diary, entries for June 9-12, 1831 (Missouri Historical Society, St. Louis); Lovejoy, *Memoir,* pp. 39-40.

intellect, and despite frequently violent opposition. "I have used the surgeon's knife ere now," said he, "when the cries and even the anger of the infant patient grieved me; but still I kept on." There were few more able religious orators anywhere in the West than Nelson, and under his influence a full-scale revival was soon taking place in St. Louis.[5]

For a period of nearly two weeks in January, 1832, revival meetings were held almost every evening in the First Presbyterian Church. Men and women of all ages and conditions came to sit in the dimly lighted sanctuary to hear themselves convicted of sin by the Reverend David Nelson, to feel his surgeon's knife probe deep. Lovejoy, remorseful for having "so long lived in sin" and having "resisted so much light," took his seat with them regularly in the hope of being converted. The chances were excellent that Nelson would win, for only sinners more hardened than Lovejoy found it easy to resist his revival methods. At last toward the end of January the event took place. Soon afterward Lovejoy, together with the rest of Nelson's forty converts, was gathered into the membership of the First Presbyterian Church. In this manner, after what Lovejoy conceived to have been a long, sin-hardened interlude in his life, he at last accepted the position for which Daniel and Elizabeth Lovejoy had patiently reared him, the role for which he had been trained by the faculty at Waterville College.[6]

Nobody considered the religious obligations of the new church members to be ended with conversion. Now they were expected to enter at once into the reform activities the clergy had designed to renovate the world. Finney, America's leading revivalist in that era, directed his own converts to devote themselves to practical Christianity—to "abolition of slavery, temperance, moral reform, politics, business principles, physiological and dietetic reform." Lovejoy pondered the problem this posed for him. Where did his own responsibility lie? Surely the St. Louis *Times,* as he and Miller currently edited it, did not fully satisfy the demands of Christian duty. He prayerfully consulted with

. . . . .

[5] Benjamin G. Merkel, "The Abolition Aspects of Missouri's Antislavery Controversy, 1819-1865," *Missouri Historical Review,* XLIV (1949-50), 239; St. Louis *Observer,* August 7, 1834.

[6] Lovejoy to his parents, February 22, 1832, Lovejoy Collection.

the Reverend William Potts for guidance. Together they concluded that duty required him to study theology in preparation for the ministry.[7]

Completely enthusiastic about the fateful turn his life had taken, Lovejoy wasted no time in beginning the new, avowedly religious phase of his career. Within two weeks he had dissolved his partnership with T. J. Miller, sold his share in the newspaper, and left St. Louis to make the long trip back East, not knowing when, if ever, he would return to Missouri.[8]

On March 24, 1832, he enrolled at Princeton Theological Seminary, the center of orthodox Presbyterianism. He took a few weeks off in the summer to travel to Maine to visit his family. But he returned to Princeton as soon as he could to spend the winter studying theology. By the next spring he had completed an academic course which ordinarily required many months longer, and the second presbytery of Philadelphia licensed him to preach as a probationer.[9]

Although he had a good record at Princeton, the young preacher had come to accept religious tenets which, had he chosen to reveal them, would have rendered him highly suspect in the eyes of many important Presbyterian churchmen of that day. Lovejoy's theology harmonized in all essentials with the views of those left-wing Presbyterians who a few years later would be called "new school." Such traces of orthodoxy as remained in his creed were overshadowed by his confidence in man's ability both to shape his own salvation and to renovate the world. In practice, however—and this was the shocking thing—Lovejoy manifested little interest in formal theology under any guise. This obviously resulted not from any deficiency of training or intellect but simply from the fact that to him religion was not a matter for dialectic but an affair of the heart whose yield ought to be measured by its social product. He thought of himself essentially as an evangelist concerned with arousing the apathetic men around him first to

. . . . .

[7] *Ibid.;* Finney quoted in Charles C. Cole, Jr., *The Social Ideas of the Northern Evangelists, 1826-1860* (New York, 1954), p. 77.

[8] St. Louis *Times,* February 18, 1832.

[9] Lovejoy to his parents, April 2, 1832, Lovejoy, *Memoir,* pp. 47-48; *Princeton Theological Seminary Biographical Catalogue, 1909* (Trenton, New Jersey, 1909), p. 105; License, April 18, 1833, Wickett-Wiswall Collection.

repentance and then to the performance of good works. Others might argue about the precise mechanism of salvation. The results which flowed from it interested Lovejoy far more than did the recondite details of its process.

Lovejoy believed man capable of going far toward producing his own salvation. He rejected altogether the view that because man had fallen the taint of original sin inclined him irremediably toward evil. "Man sins not because he *must,*" explained Lovejoy, "but because he *will* sin." He becomes a sinner only at that moment "when as a free, moral agent, he first breaks the law of God." Although nothing is easier than repentance (it is "simply a change of mind, a change of purpose"), repentance produces a complete transformation in the character of the believer who experiences it. Through the process of conversion the sin that lodges in the unbeliever's breast is undone. Endowed with holiness, he has in truth been born again. The convert's future goodness, Lovejoy explained, consists in doing good for uniformly good motives. Christians, once converted, "are to let their light shine by holy example. Without this, all their professions will be of little value—will do little good. . . . Let there be a complete symmetry of character, a perfect consistency of conduct, from one day to another. . . ." In sum, the Christian must be a reformer. As though all this were not unorthodox enough, Lovejoy also wholeheartedly accepted the use of Finney's "means" for producing revivals—means which few Eastern clergymen yet held in high repute. Characteristically, Lovejoy approved them not because of theory but solely because they worked: "the anxious seat, the inquiry room, the camp ground, &c. &c.—they may seem strange to many, but so long as souls are converted by them, we rejoice, yea, and we will rejoice."[10]

In spite of these views which ill prepared him for life in a conservative theological atmosphere, Lovejoy was tempted for a while with the idea of making a career for himself in the East. Considering everything, the East offered him an attractive future. If he were successful as a clergyman in one of the growing cities along the coast, he could certainly live well. He might even win a measure of fame and

. . . . .

[10] St. Louis *Times,* January 2, February 20, July 17, August 7, November 20, 1834.

influence by preaching sermons to large urban congregations. And if he felt so inclined, he could indulge his taste for power by entering the high councils of the church. Momentarily succumbing to these several lures, he appealed to the influential Reverend Albert Barnes, pastor of the First Presbyterian Church in Philadelphia, to help him find a suitable pulpit. Barnes, soon to become a target of religious controversy because of his liberal theology, recommended him for an appointment to Newport, Rhode Island, which he assured Lovejoy was "in many respects an important place."[11]

For a few weeks in the spring of 1833 Lovejoy preached at Newport, but deciding that "God had nothing for him to do there," he moved in June to the Spring Street Church in New York City.[12] He had made nearly as good an impression at Princeton as he had in his college days at Waterville. Now men of influence within the Presbyterian church saw fit to help him take the first steps toward what they supposed would be a successful ministerial career. They recommended him not to minor posts in country villages but to "important places" where his obvious talents and zeal could find adequate expression and reward. They pictured a future for him that would duplicate their own careers. Security and comfort could be his, with enough popular attention to be satisfying but never really dangerous. It hardly occurred to them that a product of sound theological training might aspire to something other than emulation of themselves, the statesmen of the church.

But they had miscalculated both Lovejoy and the times. Great Eastern cities no longer attracted him. Their pulpits, however important, struck him as dull and formal, their congregations spiritless. During the summer that Lovejoy preached in New York, several events convinced him of the superficiality of the East. The appearance of the Indian chief Black Hawk created a sensation among the curious; shortly afterward the populace turned out in great numbers to watch a balloon ascension; and then a crowd of 150,000 gathered to see President Andrew Jackson as he toured the city. Lovejoy witnessed each of these

. . . . .

[11] Albert Barnes to Lovejoy, June 21, 1833, Lovejoy Collection.

[12] Lovejoy, *Memoir,* p. 60; Joseph Lovejoy to Owen Lovejoy, August 6, 1833, Owen Lovejoy Papers (William L. Clements Library, University of Michigan, Ann Arbor).

events, and he confessed momentary interest. But all the pageantry and excitement, he told his mother, was "vanity, and as such I felt it at the time." Cities were artificial, Lovejoy thought; their populations had been ensnared by the delusions of the world.[13]

The West was different. To Lovejoy, who understood the impact the West must eventually have on the nation, it appeared that everything of significance happening in America was happening there. Like many another young Puritan he had become convinced that the great valley of the Mississippi formed the vast arena in which the last stages of the conflict of the ages, the final battle between good and evil, were about to be enacted. It is plain, said Lyman Beecher, the famous New England divine, "that the religious and political destiny of our nation is to be decided in the West." And not the destiny of the United States alone. The "cause of free institutions and the liberty of the world," Beecher had said, were at issue in the crossroad villages and lonely farms far across the Appalachian Mountains. Only the dull could ignore the West's vast challenge.[14]

Lovejoy's attention soon turned in that direction. For a time he had considered returning to Maine and settling near his parents' home. He soon abandoned that idea, for as he performed the polite round of his formal pastoral tasks in New York City, and when he was alone in quiet places, his conscience troubled him with a constant question: would he be fulfilling his Christian duty by remaining merely a spectator to the crucial battle that raged in the heart of America?[15]

Meanwhile, without his knowing it, the answer to the question was being framed for him by friends in St. Louis. A group of Presbyterian laymen in the city had decided the time had come to establish a reform newspaper in Missouri. Two years earlier, in the spring of 1831, another transplanted New Englander, young Andrew Benton from Connecticut, had proposed such a paper "to aid in the promotion of religion, morality and education . . . and to exert an influence in favor of the benevolent institutions of the age. . . ." But since Benton could not find financial backers, nothing had come of his plans; and not

. . . . .

[13] Lovejoy to Elizabeth Lovejoy, June 18, 1833, Wickett-Wiswall Collection.
[14] Lyman Beecher, *A Plea for the West* (Cincinnati, Ohio, 1835), p. 11.
[15] Lovejoy to his parents, August 5, 1833, Wickett-Wiswall Collection.

many months after Lovejoy had left for Princeton, Benton had gone off to Cincinnati to train for the ministry at Lane Seminary.[16] Now, in the summer of 1833, a few well-to-do men in St. Louis, under the influence of the revival, were prepared to supply money for the project. The only thing they lacked was a suitable editor. The sponsors were looking for someone who possessed editorial experience, a zeal for reform, and standing among the clergy. They soon realized that the man they wanted was in New York City.

When Lovejoy received their letter describing the new venture and inviting him to assume the post of editor, he knew he had no choice in the matter. He had planned to return to Maine in the fall to comfort his mother, for Daniel Lovejoy had died early in August. But with the letter from St. Louis in hand, the path of duty opened clearly before him. He avoided every possible distraction. A letter to his brother explained that he could not visit Maine (nor was he ever to go there again). "They are impatiently calling me to the West," he wrote in haste, "and to the West I must go."[17]

Making careful plans for his departure, he obtained an appointment from the American Home Missionary Society, which would provide the assurance of at least some financial support for his work on the Missouri frontier.[18] Probably before he left, he also visited the clergymen who had interested themselves in his career to explain to them why he felt impelled to leave the East. Whether they understood or not made no difference. Lovejoy understood, and that was enough.

. . . . .

[16] Prospectus of St. Louis *Observer* (Missouri Historical Library, St. Louis); Gilbert Hobbs Barnes, *The Antislavery Impulse, 1830-1844* (New York, 1933), p. 46.

[17] Lovejoy to Owen Lovejoy, August 26, 1833, Lovejoy, *Memoir,* p. 66.

[18] Lovejoy to Absalom Peters, February 20, 1832, American Home Missionary Society Papers (Hammond Library, Chicago Theological Seminary). Hereafter cited as AHMS Papers.

The Religious Editor

Chapter IV

Arriving once more in St. Louis, on November 12, 1833, Lovejoy started his new work with all possible speed. On November 17 he preached his first sermon as an itinerant agent for the American Home Missionary Society, and five days later issued the first number of the St. Louis *Observer*. On the masthead of the *Observer* appeared the Biblical motto, "Jesus Christ, and Him Crucified." It was a religious newspaper to serve the churches in the far West; no one could mistake that. And it was to be comprehensive in its religious purpose. The editor would devote himself, the paper announced, to "Christian politics, the diffusion of religious intelligence, and the salvation of souls."[1]

Lovejoy approached his new enterprise with a spirit of optimism common enough in 1833, but the type which few Americans have since shared. For a little while in the second quarter of the nineteenth century there was granted to some men in America a vision of the world made perfect, perhaps within their own lifetime. A particularly heady zeal impelled them, for they believed they had heard the messenger of the Lord summoning them to fight in His battle against the mighty legions of evil, and in response they had mustered the hosts of the church to conquer the entire world for Christianity.

As Lovejoy stepped off the boat that had carried him back to St. Louis, he enjoyed the comforting assurance that even at that moment

. . . . .

[1] Lovejoy to Absalom Peters, February 20, 1834, AHMS Papers; St. Louis *Observer*, January 9, 1834.

missionaries were spreading the Gospel to the remote corners of the earth, and reform was progressing everywhere. He could be certain, as a devout Presbyterian, that all things were moving toward the desired end. Earnest reformers were rescuing a lost race from the ruins of the Fall, liberty at last was besting tyranny, and the righteous were driving evil into the cramped corners of the world. In such vast enterprises the church was then engaged, and in them, he believed, she should surely triumph. Enlisted in this mighty cause, Lovejoy partook of the special assurance that comes only to those hostages of history who can be certain that time is on their side. It is the kind of certainty that invites a man to hazard much, to be heedless of the opposition of the unconsecrated, and even, if need be, to risk martyrdom.[2]

In that first autumn and winter back in the West, Lovejoy was busier than he had ever been before. There seemed no limit to his energies as he absorbed himself completely in religion and reform. Every Thursday he had to bring out the newspaper. Between publication days, in keeping with his appointment from the American Home Missionary Society, he rode out from St. Louis over primitive roads and through all kinds of weather to hold religious services for the yeoman farmers who were either too scattered or too poor to support their own church and pastor. Whenever he could assemble enough people, he preached and held singing schools. Where the religious sentiment seemed particularly strong, he organized temperance societies and Bible societies. During the long weekends as he rode alone on horseback through the wooded solitudes of eastern Missouri, he thought out the editorials he would write as soon as he had returned to his desk. With half his time spent in preaching and half in running the newspaper, his life became a never-ending round of activity, his days so filled with duties that when he came back to town in the middle of the week to put the *Observer* together, he seldom got to bed before two o'clock in the morning. The few spare hours left from this routine he devoted to reform societies—and not simply to passive membership. He was soon made an agent of the American Sunday School Union

. . . . .

[2] Edward D. Griffin, "Sermon Preached September 14, 1826, Before the American Board of Missions, at Middletown, Connecticut," *The National Preacher,* I (1826-27), 62-64; "On Public Spirit," *American Baptist Magazine,* VI (1826), 80-85; Lovejoy, *Memoir,* pp. 69-70, 78-81.

and elected treasurer and agent of the Missouri and Illinois Tract Society, treasurer of the Missouri Bible Society, and treasurer (later corresponding secretary) of the Missouri Sunday School Union.[3]

Since religious activity presented its special difficulties in the 1830's, it would have been too much to expect that Lovejoy's projects could have proceeded smoothly and without controversy. Religious institutions everywhere in America seemed to be in flux. In that time of theological change, doctrine mattered a great deal, and serious doctrinal differences appeared especially among Presbyterians. Already the Presbyterian church was filled with those tensions between conservatives and liberals that would shortly split the church into old-school and new-school factions. No Presbyterian editor could avoid the conflict. Powerful members of the church, Lovejoy found, urged him to present points of view in the *Observer* that other members fought to have suppressed. He could write practically nothing that did not bring a letter in an early mail from someone who objected. "Keen-eyed orthodoxy," he complained, watched his every movement; "sharp-scented, long-winded bigotry" constantly dogged his tracks. Clearly his own sympathies lay with the liberal members of the church who emphasized man's ability to aid in producing his own salvation and who advocated the generous use of revivals and reform societies. But every time he revealed his views, he drew down the wrath of the opposition. In the summer of 1834 he rode over to the little town of Fayette to preach to a small audience in the courthouse. After he had started his sermon, a man in the congregation, displeased with Lovejoy's unorthodox statements, left his seat, marched to the door, and just before stepping outside, turned around and yelled out David Crockett's old motto at full voice, "Be sure you are right, and then, go ahead."[4]

Not only did division appear within the Presbyterian church, there were major differences, too, among the several Protestant denominations in Missouri. Since the *Observer,* a Presbyterian newspaper, displayed some interest in politics, complications easily resulted. In the summer of 1834, Lovejoy printed the slate of candidates for sheriff of

. . . . .

[3] Lovejoy to Absalom Peters, March 11, 1835, AHMS Papers; St. Louis *Observer,* January 23, June 5, 1834.

[4] St. Louis *Observer,* March 6, July 10, 1834.

St. Louis, listing Nathan Ranney's name first. Because Ranney was an elder in the First Presbyterian Church and active in the Presbyterian-dominated reform societies, sensitive members of other denominations complained that Lovejoy showed favoritism and was trying to promote a Presbyterian scheme to control the sheriff's office.[5]

So much contention might have suggested that Lovejoy's enterprises exercised great influence in Missouri. He knew better. Only a small circle of religious controversialists paid any real attention to him, and this was true in spite of the endless hours he devoted to preaching, to reform societies, and to his newspaper. His missionary work had started out well enough. Indeed, a man less sanguine than Lovejoy might have been satisfied with the little congregations that gathered each week, listened politely to his pleas for repentance and reform, and joined his temperance societies. But the results were far less than Lovejoy had expected. He himself was thoroughly dedicated to his task and convinced that he bore a message for a world in need. The world, however, merely ignored him. The work-hardened farmers and their wives who came to hear his sermons were never ignited into revival by the religious firebrands he tossed at them from behind his improvised pulpits. "The work of the Lord ceases," he wrote, "while the work of destruction goes bravely on."[6]

The story of the *Observer* was not much different. It, too, brought little but discouragement. Although it was a well-edited newspaper whose content could stand comparison with similar religious journals in New York and Cincinnati, the fact remained that its potential audience was sharply limited by its place of publication. Baptists, Methodists, and (in St. Louis) Catholics composed the majority of the area's churchgoing population. There simply were not many Presbyterians in Missouri and Illinois, and still fewer of them were of the new-school variety. At the end of the first month of publication the *Observer*'s circulation remained so small that few people could have known it existed. Every week its backers lost thirty dollars from the enterprise, a sum they were unwilling to sink indefinitely. They soon let Lovejoy know that unless he could secure more subscribers the *Observer*, on whose service to the reform cause he had counted so much, would pres-

. . . . .

[5] *Ibid.*, July 17, 1834.
[6] *Ibid.*, July 31, 1834.

ently fail. Even by midsummer, 1834, Lovejoy still had only 700 subscribers, and many of them neglected to pay the subscription fee. He could secure few advertisements and constantly fell deeper into debt.[7]

When the winter of 1833-34 had passed and a soggy spring had come again to St. Louis, Lovejoy paused for a time to assess his achievements, as men sometimes must do. What he discovered caused him to sink into one of those depressive moods that had so often possessed him. Now in the thirty-second year of his age, he thought he had every reason to count himself a failure. Solemnly dedicating his life to the cause of religion and moral reform, he had sacrificed the prospect of worldly success to return to Missouri. But of what avail were all his efforts? He worked in a region where New England ideals were not appreciated, and his newspaper was scarcely noticed in Missouri or anywhere else. "The vicissitudes of life are nothing but a series of disappointments," he reflected soon afterward. "Whether for good or for ill, none of all our ten thousand cherished plans have succeeded exactly to our wish."[8] The people around St. Louis were too absorbed with making money, he decided, to be interested in sustaining a religious publication. Nor did his preaching prove much more effective. He had brought few men to conversion, had started no revivals. Of all his reform efforts, he thought wryly, only his temperance work flourished. Such success, after all, provided but small comfort, for he knew well enough that the few temperance societies he could organize among the farmers in Missouri would do little to save a lost humanity.[9]

He was "perplexed a thousand ways," he confessed, and unable to preach or to write as he ought to do. Finally in his discouragement he decided he must leave St. Louis, and appealed to the American Home Missionary Society to transfer him to Kentucky, where he supposed a Presbyterian reformer would find a more appreciative audience. The Society, however, needing agents not in hospitable areas but in places where reformers met obstacles, ignored his request. Since without their

. . . . .

[7] *Ibid.*, July 17, 1834; Lovejoy to John F. Brooks, December 26, 1833 (Chicago Historical Society); E. O. Howard to Lovejoy, October 27, 1834, Wickett-Wiswall Collection.

[8] St. Louis *Observer*, August 28, 1834; Lovejoy to Elizabeth Lovejoy, June 3, 1834, Wickett-Wiswall Collection.

[9] Lovejoy to Absalom Peters, July 24, August 21, 1834, AHMS Papers.

aid Lovejoy could not move, he dutifully remained at his post in St. Louis, preaching and writing but convinced, nonetheless, that his work was practically useless, that the *Observer* must presently go under, submerged by the worldliness and indifference that flourished there on the edge of the frontier. Never did he doubt, even in the darkest hour, that the armies of the Lord would eventually prevail; but he perhaps often asked himself how many casualties they must suffer before the victory was won at last.[10]

During that bleak summer of 1834 Lovejoy allowed only the slightest intimation of his internal conflict to reach the pages of the *Observer*. The newspaper continued to reflect the buoyancy of the era's religious optimism, and Lovejoy himself maintained his usual interest in reform. Such doubts as he certainly felt concerning his own efficacy did not extend to a questioning of the tenets of the religious reformer's creed. Indeed, as the months passed, his reform ideas, hitherto diffuse, began to find focus. Out of Lovejoy's melancholy came his recognition of that important principle of action which the history of humanitarianism suggests—a successful reformer does not merely wish all men well; he directs his energy toward specifics. "If good to our fellow creatures is to be accomplished," Lovejoy wrote, "it must be, not by vague resolutions, but by a steady persevering purpose, formed under a sense of our responsibility to God."[11] Probably Charles Finney or David Nelson or William Potts could have told him as much, but Lovejoy discovered it for himself, which perhaps strengthened the lesson.

For the first six months that Lovejoy edited the *Observer,* he had filled his columns with essays and letters on conventional themes, chiefly theological and moral. Although the newspaper was clearly permeated with the attitude of liberal Presbyterianism, it had contained few surprises. Insofar as Lovejoy concentrated on any specific social need, he had been interested in the temperance crusade; even before leaving New England, he had thought hard liquor one of society's most vicious enemies. But mature reflection soon convinced him that he should move on to battle other, more formidable foes.[12]

. . . . .

[10] *Ibid.*

[11] St. Louis *Observer,* November 20, 1834.

[12] Journal of Elijah P. Lovejoy, Lovejoy Collection.

In the summer of 1834, following the pattern of evolutionary development typical of pre–Civil War reformers, he began to write—and in a less cautious manner—about slavery and the dangers of "popery." As his ideas on these subjects clarified and his views became more extreme, a change took place both in him and in his reading public. Soon he had completely changed his mind about leaving St. Louis. In the fall his brother, eighteen-year-old John Ellingwood, came out from Maine to join him and learn the printer's trade. It was a sign that in the eyes of the Lovejoy family, Elijah had at last attained position in the world. No longer need he think of himself as a failure in promoting the cause of God, although the storm he created by his writing threatened momentarily to overwhelm him.

A storm it was, for the indifference that had greeted the *Observer* at its appearance and accompanied it during its first months of publication was gradually replaced by active hostility. Missourians who had hardly known of Lovejoy's presence in St. Louis soon realized that a stern Puritan dwelt among them, and they were made uncomfortably aware that from his press every week issued a challenging reform newspaper.

From the day he distributed the first issue of the *Observer* in the streets of St. Louis, Lovejoy had never given his readers any reason to suppose that he would be easy to get along with, or that the *Observer* would prove to be a comfort to the complacent. The first editorial he wrote had promised that although the newspaper would "seek no controversy," neither would it decline any. "Truth . . . in all its severity" was to be its aim. And while Lovejoy hoped to arrive at that goal peacefully, he would do so, he announced, only insofar "as that is consistent with the defence of the Truth." Whatever the consequences, he warned his readers, the *Observer* would "never shrink from the post of duty; nor fear to speak out. . . ."[13]

For nearly a year Lovejoy's search for the severity of Truth had not upset anyone very much. His condemnations of such lapses from propriety as Sabbath breaking, blasphemy, and the use of tobacco and whiskey were expected from the editor of a religious journal. Articles on such subjects produced little discord, arousing no more resentment

. . . . .

[13] St. Louis *Observer,* November 22, 1833.

among the public than an easygoing husband might feel toward his newly converted wife who set herself to the task of reforming him. Probably few readers, for example, were greatly disturbed when, reading Lovejoy's account of his walk down Front Street in St. Louis, they learned that "one thing" had depressed his spirits—"It was the moral condition of a large portion of those whom I saw. . . . The drunkeries and drinking I witnessed, the oaths and the obscene blasphemies I heard, caused my spirits to sink within me." Nor is it likely that many were as conscience-stricken as he to find milk carts and bread carts doing business in the city streets on Sunday.[14]

The *Observer*'s early articles against the Catholic church, written by a correspondent who signed himself "Waldo," were not particularly noticed either, though they began appearing practically as soon as the *Observer* was established. Of course, opposition to "popery" was already an old story by 1834. Protestants had long professed to believe that the Pope in connivance with various European monarchs had arranged a vast plot to win the American West for despotic government and Roman Catholicism. As early as 1830 the American Bible Society and the American Education Society had warned Americans that the Catholic church was about to seize control of the Mississippi valley. The *Observer* merely followed the trend. Yet Lovejoy's location alone would probably have been sufficient to prompt him, a zealous, evangelical Protestant, to crusading anti-Catholicism, for St. Louis was the most important Catholic center in the Mississippi valley north of New Orleans. One-third of its population was Catholic, a Jesuit college had recently been founded there, and the city served as headquarters for many Catholic activities in the West. Here the power of the Catholic church was tangible and growing. Lovejoy felt compelled to state the grounds for his opposition.[15]

At first few could have been shocked by the running controversy he carried on in his newspaper over the merits of Catholicism. Lovejoy's Protestant readers expected to find such material in a religious newspaper; and though the Catholic weekly, *The Shepherd of the Valley,*

. . . . .

[14] "Letter from the Editor, May 21, 1835," Lovejoy, *Memoir,* pp. 129-130; St. Louis *Observer,* February 27, 1834.

[15] Ray Allen Billington, *The Protestant Crusade, 1800-1860, a Study of the Origins of American Nativism* (New York, 1938), pp. 32-76.

sometimes replied to his accusations, few Catholic laymen read the *Observer*.[16] For months Lovejoy did not write against the Catholic church himself, but as opposition to "Waldo's" articles appeared and as he read copies of the New York *Protestant Vindicator,* he became personally anti-Catholic. He was encouraged in this course by Edwin F. Hatfield, the young pastor of the Second Presbyterian Church, whom Lovejoy later called his "file leader" in the "Papish conflict." "We have broken our truce with this spirit of darkness," Lovejoy finally announced. "Henceforth we stand in direct and unceasing and uncompromising hostility to it. . . . We were loath to believe—what we are now fully convinced of—that it is a spirit of unmixed evil."[17]

The *Observer*'s anti-Catholicism gradually intensified. Soon it abandoned merely theoretical criticism and began to strike close to home. In October, 1834, the Roman Catholic cathedral in St. Louis, one of the largest buildings west of the Appalachians, was consecrated in a magnificent ceremony in which a United States military band from Jefferson Barracks took part, "with fife, and drum, and clarionet, and bassoon." It was a Sunday morning, and Protestant sensibilities were outraged when at half-past ten, just as church services were starting, "the cannons' mouths began to roar" and continued, reported the *Observer's* correspondent, "for half an hour." Lovejoy used that event, of which Catholics were understandably proud, as the occasion for printing "Waldo's" particularly strong condemnation of the Catholic church, whose power in St. Louis was obviously considerable.[18] Soon his Whig political preference led him to attack the local Irish immigrants and members of the Democratic party, many of whom also were Catholic. Catholic opposition to him rapidly became bitter. "I venture to predict your speedy extinction as an Editor in St. Louis," wrote one Catholic. "The people will not patronize a slanderer, a calumniator, a libeller." The most violent name calling appeared in an open letter from the Catholic "P.B." to "Mr. Love-Joy, Alias LOVE- . . . . .

[16] "Elijah P. Lovejoy as an Anti-Catholic," *Records of the American Catholic Historical Society of Philadelphia,* LXII (September, 1951), 172-175; St. Louis *Observer,* January 2, 9, and 16, April 10, May 1, 8, and 22, June 5, July 10, September 4, 1834.

[17] Lovejoy to Hatfield, January 21, 1836 (Massachusetts Historical Society, Boston); St. Louis *Observer,* September 4, 1834.

[18] St. Louis *Observer,* October 30, 1834.

Lies!!" charging him with the "noble appellation of forger and slanderer" and characterizing his writings as "malicious inventions" produced by a "polluted hand."[19]

Inevitably Lovejoy was soon branded as bigoted, fanatic, intolerant, and quarrelsome, even by men less hysterical than "P.B." And all those adjectives could be properly applied. Yet in condemning the Catholic church, he only followed the course his conscience told him was right, and no good man could do less. Lovejoy belonged to that species of New England Puritan whose representatives have always supposed that God speaks to them more intimately than He speaks to ordinary men. In that reform age, they felt a special obligation to attempt to understand His will. They struggled mightily to grasp the Truth, and having once attained it, they could be swayed by no contrary influence, for they knew with certainty that they were right. Toleration and compromise were not ordinarily parts of their intellectual equipment.

In the minds of such men in the 1830's the Catholic church was synonymous with ignorance, immorality, and despotism, all of which they were duty-bound to oppose. Consequently as they watched in fear the growing power of the Catholic church in the United States, they determined in the name of their version of Truth to do everything possible to limit its influence.

Lovejoy tried to explain to less committed men why he persisted in his rash, unpopular course against the Catholic church. "We believe the cause of Truth, demands it," he wrote simply. Since not many people in St. Louis understood what he was talking about, he continued to search for language powerful enough to convey to them his idea of the danger the country faced from Catholicism. Unfortunately for the serenity of St. Louis he found the words he sought. He had seen, he wrote, "the stealthy, cat-like step, the hyena grin, with which the 'Mother of Abominations,' was approaching the Fountain of Protestant Liberty, that she might cast into it the poison of her incantations, more accursed than was ever seethed in the Caldron of Hecate."[20]

Such intemperate statements were certain to produce a reaction . . . . .

[19] *Shepherd of the Valley,* February 28, 1834, August 29, 1835, cited in "Elijah P. Lovejoy as an Anti-Catholic," p. 174.

[20] St. Louis *Observer,* June 11, August 27, 1835.

dangerous to their author. Although Eastern editors could use such language with impunity, it was not possible to do so in St. Louis. When Protestant newspapers in Philadelphia or New York published similar attacks, they issued them in communities dominated by Protestants. In St. Louis, however, the Catholic element was both large and influential, the Protestant element small. In other cities it was the Catholic church that suffered from the wrath of the Protestants; in St. Louis the Catholics rebelled against Lovejoy. By the fall of 1835, his persistent criticism had aroused so much ill feeling among the Catholics in Missouri that it was clear they would be happy to be rid of so great a trouble maker.

In spite of this turmoil, however, Lovejoy as yet had been given no reason to think his situation dangerous. There was, in fact, cause to be optimistic as Protestants began to recognize the potential power of their new advocate. In the fall of 1834, the Presbyterian synods of Missouri and Illinois had recommended the *Observer* to the patronage of church members, and a large group of agents—eleven in Illinois alone—began work in both states to sell subscriptions to the *Observer*.[21]

With more money coming in and his influence spreading, Lovejoy thought his position improved to the extent that he could establish a home and family of his own. During the winter while the religious controversy raged, he found time to court Celia Ann French, daughter of a farmer in the nearby village of St. Charles, and on March 4, 1835, they were married. He was thirty-two, she eleven years younger. While Celia sat beside him at his desk, he penned a rapturous letter to his mother announcing the marriage and describing his bride. "She is," he wrote, "tall, well-shaped, of a light, fair complexion, dark flaxen hair, large blue eyes, with features of a perfect Grecian contour. In short, she is *very beautiful*."[22]

Though Celia Lovejoy's piety could easily match her husband's, she never shared his intellectual interest in reform and took no part in his public life. Nevertheless she encouraged him to take a strong stand for the cause he believed right, and she bore the ordeals it brought her

. . . . .

[21] *Ibid.*, November 13 and 27, 1835; Minutes of the Synod of Illinois, New School, 1831-69, I, 50 (Virginia Library, McCormick Theological Seminary, Chicago).

[22] Lovejoy to Elizabeth Lovejoy, March 10, 1835, Lovejoy, *Memoir*, pp. 132-133.

with patience and fortitude. One cannot suppose that their brief married life together was productive of much happiness for her. Members of her family soon expressed hostility toward her husband and the cause he had espoused, she herself was ill much of the time, they were soon poorer than they had expected to be, and her husband's public affairs moved from one nerve-racking crisis to another, leaving her at last a widow at the age of twenty-four.[23]

Even at the time of their marriage the situation was developing that would eventually make their position in St. Louis untenable. Soon opponents of Lovejoy's ideas would refuse to tolerate him and his newspaper any longer. It was not Catholics alone, however, who found the *Observer* disturbing during 1835. While Lovejoy continued to publish the articles that fomented religious discord in the city, his conscience was leading him also to take a strong stand against slavery.

He could not avoid committing himself on so momentous a subject. By the time he began publishing the *Observer,* the roll of abolition thunder already reverberated across the land. Liberal Presbyterians throughout the North and West were among the leaders of the abolition movement. For Lovejoy to ignore the issue was impossible.

. . . . .

[23] Celia Lovejoy to Elizabeth Lovejoy, April 10, 1841, Wickett-Wiswall Collection.

Toward Abolition

Chapter V

From some points of view, slavery in the United States was not the altogether evil institution that critics like Lovejoy pictured. As Southerners had begun to point out in the 1820's, slavery had been the means of giving a backward people some of the elements of Christian civilization. And it was also true, as apologists were fond of noting, that the slaves were about as well supplied with food, clothing, and shelter as many white Americans, and that they enjoyed a degree of security in sickness and old age unknown to the Northern industrial worker.

The abolitionists themselves might have admitted the truth of all these claims, but there remained one consideration so fundamental that in their opinion it cancelled out every good thing that could be said about slavery—the slave was not free. He might enjoy all sorts of privileges, and his material comforts might be many, but he possessed none of the rights God intended man to have. He could not enjoy the fruits of his own labor. He could not enjoy the domestic relations of marriage and parenthood. He could not so regulate his conduct as to prepare his immortal soul for eternity. He had, in short, been degraded from a human being, the child of God, to the position of a chattel, a thing.

To those people in the United States who valued individual liberty and religion above everything else, such arguments were decisive. It did not matter to them how indulgently the master might treat his slave. The irreducible fact remained that he *was* a slave. On the implications drawn from this premise they based their attack on slavery.[1]

Of course opposition to slavery was already well developed by the time Lovejoy began to write about it in 1834. Indeed, organized opposition to the institution dated from at least the foundation of the Republic. During the post-Revolutionary period many important men, both in the North and in the South, had shared a dislike for slavery, and antislavery societies based on much the same broad humanitarian grounds as the Revolution itself had then flourished in both sections of the country. In 1817 Northern and Southern philanthropists had cooperated to form the American Colonization Society, which was designed to encourage manumissions by arranging to transport the freed Negroes to Africa. The colonization society had thus recognized the greatest obstacle to the success of any scheme of emancipation that might be proposed—racial prejudice. Most people in that day believed Negroes to be biologically inferior to white men. How then, they often asked, could the two races live together in harmony and safety without the institution of slavery to keep the inferior race in subjection? In spite of that problem, which perplexed even the wisest, the generation of Americans living in 1800 supposed that some day a solution would be found, and slavery would eventually die out.[2]

The controversy over the admission of Missouri to the Union as a slave state had changed all that. Whatever remained in the second decade of the nineteenth century of the genial assurance that slavery would die a natural death, was ended by that dispute in 1819 and 1820. Northerners who had comfortably thought of slavery as a decadent institution now saw it as a dynamic force seeking to extend itself across the West. Southerners who had been apologetic for slavery now considered themselves citizens of a besieged minority section. While their slave property increased in value each year as new Western lands were turned to the production of cotton, they began to defend the institution they had once deplored.

. . . . .

[1] See, for example, "What are the Doctrines of Anti-Slavery Men?," Alton *Observer,* July 20, 1837.

[2] Dwight Lowell Dumond, "Race Prejudice and Abolition, New Views on the Antislavery Movement," *Michigan Alumnus Quarterly Review,* XLI (April, 1935), 377-385.

Despite this changed attitude the decade of the 1820's was a time of relative quiet on the subject of slavery. The American Colonization Society, looking more and more like a proslavery organization, continued its hopeless efforts to remove the free Negroes. A few dedicated humanitarians such as the quiet Quaker editor, Benjamin Lundy, continued to spread antislavery ideas and to organize antislavery societies in the North and the upper South. Nevertheless, the voices raised against slavery in the 1820's were neither loud nor insistent nor much heeded, and the prospect that slavery would ever be ended in the United States receded farther and farther into the background.

But by 1830 the period of quiet was over, and no one could really believe it would ever come again. Throughout the Northern states a new spirit moved. The New England conscience, nurtured by generations of theologians in the tradition of benevolence, had at last begun to act. In western New York the Reverend Charles G. Finney had led a generation of young men down the path of religious revival onto the fields of reform where many of them were to spend their lives crusading against slavery. In New York City Arthur and Lewis Tappan, wealthy philanthropists, stood ready to pour their sizable fortunes into reform projects. In England the well-publicized movement was underway that would lead in 1833 to the abolition of slavery in the West Indies. And in Boston on January 1, 1831, William Lloyd Garrison published the first issue of the *Liberator,* his newspaper dedicated to the immediate abolition of slavery.

Thus at the time Elijah Lovejoy began to publish the *Observer,* a new phase of the American antislavery movement had already developed. In the month David Nelson converted Lovejoy in the First Presbyterian Church in St. Louis, Garrison had organized the New England Anti-Slavery Society on a platform of immediate, uncompensated emancipation. In October, 1833, as Lovejoy prepared to leave New York City to return to Missouri, the Tappan brothers organized the New York City Anti-Slavery Society in the Chatham Street Chapel while a proslavery mob raged in the street outside. Two months later, just after Lovejoy had returned to St. Louis, representatives of the New York group of abolitionists, the Philadelphia Quakers, and Garrison's New England society formed the American Anti-Slavery Society at Philadelphia.

The increased antislavery activity opened an era of aggravated controversy. Inevitably Southerners raised vigorous objections to the abolitionists' bold criticism of their most cherished and most profitable institution. In the North antislavery men quarreled among themselves over exactly how they should proceed in their campaign to end slavery, while they aroused wrath in their own section from cautious men who regretted that the agitation had ever begun. Lovejoy's reaction to all this was different from what one might have predicted.

For years Lovejoy's Whiggish views had allowed him little sympathy for those same Southern politicians who by 1830 were defending slavery, and no sympathy at all for slavery itself. It was a curse upon the nation, he agreed, a perpetual witness to the sins of past generations and a burden to men then living. Every moral and religious consideration demanded that reformers work for its rapid extinction. Nonetheless, he at first opposed the abolitionists with nearly as much vigor as any other resident of a slave state. He considered them "the worst enemies the poor slaves have" and thought they were "riveting the chains they seek to break."[3]

Like many another antislavery man, Lovejoy had long approved of the work of the American Colonization Society. He knew at first hand the condition of free Negroes in Missouri and in Eastern cities. Society seemed to have no place for them, they were forced to live under wretched conditions, and they suffered constant degradation and discrimination. It would be better for all concerned, an act of Christian benevolence, Lovejoy thought, if they could be sent back to Africa as the American Colonization Society proposed. Therefore, when he read abolitionist charges that the colonization society was a useless organization perpetuating slavery rather than ending it, he found the idea a hard one to accept.[4]

Lovejoy had been studying at Princeton when Garrison launched

. . . . .

[3] St. Louis *Observer*, May 15 and 29, 1834; Lovejoy to his mother, February 14, 1834, Lovejoy to Joseph Lovejoy, November 21, 1834, Wickett-Wiswall Collection.

[4] St. Louis *Observer*, January 30, May 15, June 26, July 3, 1834; Alton *Observer*, February 27, 1837; Lovejoy, *Memoir*, pp. 118, 121.

his most determined attack against the colonizationists. He read Garrison's critical pamphlet, *Thoughts on Colonization,* and was not convinced by the argument. During those same months Lovejoy engaged in discussions and debates with other students at the seminary in which he regularly took the antiabolitionist side. Perhaps he had adapted himself too readily to life in a slave state to be able to accept so devastating a critique of slavery and colonization as Garrison and other abolitionists presented. Whatever the reason, Lovejoy reacted to Garrison with a degree of intemperance hardly equalled by slaveowners themselves. "An incendiary fanatic," he called him, a "weak, sick-brained and wicked disturber of the public peace . . . not only crazy but wicked," "a dishonest man." Lovejoy criticized Garrison's *Thoughts* as "one tissue of falsehoods and misrepresentations." Garrison had lived in a slave state, Lovejoy observed, and must therefore have known that he told lies about slavery. "How can you hold communion with such a foul-mouthed fellow?" he asked his brother Joseph. "Is he not a perfect blackguard?"[5]

These strictures did not mean that Lovejoy defended slavery, although his antiabolitionism made him appear to come perilously close to doing so. His comments do suggest, however, that he found the institution less repugnant than did Garrison, and they reflect a measure of toleration toward slavery—if not toward its critics. Lovejoy never actually approved of slavery—few New Englanders could. He saw much in the system to deplore. But at first it was the effects of slavery that he criticized rather than the institution itself. Lovejoy was inclined to reason with his heart where slavery was concerned. He thought of it not as an abstraction but as a system which warped the human beings involved in it and caused them to suffer.

Compared with Lovejoy, many Eastern abolitionists were bundles of cold intellect. The bullying that slave boys were often forced to endure distressed him, but this was nothing in comparison with the pain he felt when confronted with evidences of the cruelty of the domestic slave trade. Of course, even many otherwise ardent defenders of slavery dared to criticize that aspect of the system, with its inevitable

. . . . .

[5] Philadelphia *National Enquirer,* November 23, 1837; Lovejoy to Elizabeth Lovejoy, April 1, 1833, Lovejoy to Joseph Lovejoy, November 21, 1834, Wickett-Wiswall Collection.

separation of husband from wife, of children from parents. On one occasion in St. Louis Lovejoy heard of the sorrow of a young slave near the city whose wife had been bought by a trader. The situation aroused Lovejoy's indignation. He wrote a passionate letter to the *Missouri Republican* protesting the event. The slave husband's face may not be white, observed Lovejoy—who was himself at that time still unmarried—but "his blood is as red and as warm as your own." As for the slave trader, Lovejoy urged his readers to "set the seal of public abhorrence and detestation upon the wretch who will thus DARE to insult the moral sense of our community and trample on the tenderest and holiest feelings of human nature." Lovejoy apparently saw no incongruity in his reference to the "moral sense" of the people of St. Louis, whom he seems to have expected to tolerate slavery while at the same time they opposed some of slavery's necessary concomitants. However much Garrison may have exaggerated slavery's evils, he would hardly have fallen into that particular trap.[6]

Lovejoy's opposition to slavery in 1834, although genuine, was thus compromised by his similar opposition to the abolitionists. He had hoped that benevolent men in all parts of the country would co-operate to end slavery. If that were to be accomplished, the good will of Southerners ought to be cultivated; they should not be deliberately antagonized. While Lovejoy often resorted to the use of harsh language himself, he objected to its use by the abolitionists. The columns of the abolitionist press were studded with such epithets as "robbers" and "murderers" applied to slaveholders. Was that kind of language calculated to win the support of the men who had the power to end slavery themselves? Lovejoy thought not. He met slaveowners daily and knew how bitterly they resented the charges of the abolitionists. In their opinion, and in his, nothing could be gained by antagonizing the South.[7]

Moreover, at first he refused to accept the accuracy of the picture the most extreme abolitionists painted of slavery. Although the institution as Lovejoy had observed it in the area around St. Louis might possess much that was pathetic and even tragic, it was not especially

. . . . .

[6] *Missouri Republican,* February 10, 1834; St. Louis *Observer,* February 13, 1834; Lovejoy to Elizabeth Lovejoy, February 14, 1834, Wickett-Wiswall Collection.

[7] St. Louis *Observer,* May 15, August 7, 1834.

brutal, and he found it hard to believe that Americans in the nineteenth century could treat their fellowmen as badly as abolitionists charged. He was not, therefore, favorably impressed with the "overstrained and highly wrought picture" of slavery presented by the students at Lane Seminary during their well-publicized eighteen-day debate over the relative merits of abolition and colonization in February, 1834. Never in the five years he had lived in Missouri had he seen or even heard of such a case of cruelty as the Lane students asserted commonly occurred. Some of the "zealous and heated young men" at the seminary, he suspected, had simply fallen "under the temptation that it would be popular to make a good speech. . . ."[8]

Lovejoy readily agreed that slavery should be ended, and the sooner the better; "but how to get rid of it, here is the difficulty," he concluded. He did not realize at first that Southerners would fail utterly to take any steps to end slavery themselves and would resist criticism of the institution to the point of violence. Amidst the claims and counterclaims of abolitionists and colonizationists, he could not immediately decide which party was right. Lovejoy, who spent so much of his time composing essays ridiculing the papacy for its claims to infallibility, decided that he would not set himself up as an authority who carried in his vest pocket the perfect solution to the problem of slavery in the United States.

His early reservations about the principles and methods of Eastern antislavery men did not last long. Having once begun a serious examination of the subject, he moved rapidly toward accepting the doctrines of the abolitionists. Continued reflection and the impact of national events would no doubt have proved sufficient in themselves to change his ideas; but there were two men in eastern Missouri during the summer of 1834 who probably helped him to make up his mind.

One of them was young Andrew Benton, who had once planned to establish the reform newspaper in St. Louis that Lovejoy edited. Now he had returned home from the tumultuous year at Lane Seminary during which he became a thorough abolitionist. He had taken a leading part in the famous student debate at Lane in February, had been elected recording secretary of the student antislavery society, and

. . . . .

[8] *Ibid.*, May 15, June 19, 1834.

finally left the seminary rather than submit to the board of trustees' dictates to cease all discussion of slavery. When he returned to St. Louis in the summer of 1834, he came as manager of the American Anti-Slavery Society for the state of Missouri. Benton had associated at Lane with Theodore D. Weld, William T. Allan, and other antislavery crusaders. He was himself a notable representative of that blend of revivalism and abolitionism which would soon convulse the Northern states. It would have been strange indeed had these two Presbyterian reformers not sought each other out—Lovejoy to obtain from Benton a first-hand account of the Lane debates and to hear from an avowed abolitionist a statement of the aims and methods of the American Anti-Slavery Society; Benton to try to influence a competent and potentially influential newspaper editor to take up the cause of abolition.[9]

Lovejoy's work for the Presbyterian church brought him into frequent contact that same summer with the Reverend David Nelson, the fiery evangelist who had been instrumental in Lovejoy's conversion two years earlier. The circumstance of their original meeting naturally made Nelson a figure of more than ordinary significance to Lovejoy. Since that day in 1833 Nelson had become increasingly interested in the slavery problem. He had long disliked slavery, and under the influence of an agent for the American Colonization Society had freed his slaves before moving from Kentucky to Missouri. Now, like so many other Presbyterian clergymen in the West, he was nearly ready to become an avowed abolitionist.[10]

In 1834 and 1835 Nelson, Benton, and Lovejoy followed the path that led from mild antislavery sentiment and faith in the program of the American Colonization Society to a rejection of both in favor of the immediate abolition of slavery. Lovejoy's hesitancy, the result perhaps as much of his geographic isolation as of his temperament, was probably counteracted by the influence of Nelson and Benton. Both men, Lovejoy recognized, held religious ideas similar to his own. Each of them could have reminded the other of their common con-

. . . . .

[9] Barnes, *Antislavery Impulse*, p. 46; American Anti-Slavery Society, *First Annual Report* (New York, 1834), pp. 135-136.

[10] William Buell Sprague, *Annals of the American Pulpit* (New York, 1859-69), IV, 686; American Anti-Slavery Society, Committee on Agencies, Minutes (Boston Public Library); *Dictionary of American Biography*, XIII, 415.

viction that man was a benevolent creature whose virtue consisted of doing good to his fellows. No field in the 1830's appeared to offer a greater opportunity for putting that principle into effect than the antislavery movement.

But for Lovejoy the path toward abolitionism was a hard one to take, and despite the influence of Nelson and Benton, he made his way cautiously during the summer and fall of 1834. Like so many other opponents of slavery it was his hope that Southerners themselves would eventually abolish the institution. Their failure to do so was chiefly responsible for his becoming an abolitionist. He thought early in the summer that he could see some steps being taken toward accomplishing what he called "the great national work" of emancipation. In October word reached him that antislavery men in Boone County, Missouri, were circulating a petition asking for an amendment to the state constitution that would gradually end slavery. Here was a way for humanitarians to end slavery without affiliating with the national antislavery movement, some of whose leaders Lovejoy still distrusted. He enthusiastically invited readers of his newspaper to contribute letters discussing the proposal. But the letters failed to come in, and to Lovejoy's regret nothing more was heard of the plan.[11]

As he read more widely in antislavery publications and watched proslavery sentiment developing in his own state, he began to realize that most people in the South were not willing to take any action to end slavery, even in the remote future. "There is a great and a very criminal apathy of feeling among the Christians of Missouri," he lamented, "as it respects the present and prospective condition of our slaves." But, he added, in spite of the apathy of Southerners, "the cause of emancipation is of God, and must prevail."[12]

The extent of the opposition of some Southerners toward even the mildest sort of sympathy for slaves or free Negroes was brought home to Lovejoy during the summer of 1834. A group of women in St. Louis, inspired by the benevolence of the time, had organized a Sunday school to which they invited Negroes. To Lovejoy's great distress the St. Louis *Times* printed an editorial implying that the "enraged . . . . .

[11] St. Louis *Observer,* July 3, October 30, November 27, 1834; Lovejoy to Joseph Lovejoy, November 21, 1834, Wickett-Wiswall Collection.

[12] St. Louis *Observer,* November 27, December 18, 1834.

multitude" ought to use mob violence to close the school, a project which the *Times* charged had been created by abolitionist influence.[13] Lovejoy's sense of fairness and Christian duty led him to write a bold defense of both the school and of abolitionists. He, too, he said, deprecated the "inconsiderate and headstrong course of the Eastern abolitionists," but the great body of them, he maintained (thinking perhaps of Nelson and Benton), were men "who claim respect alike for their piety and their general intelligence." The abolitionists were probably mistaken, he conceded, in trying to end slavery immediately. Yet, he added, "slavery as it now exists among us must cease to exist. There can be no doubt on this subject; God, and man . . . alike forbid its perpetuity."

It was cruel and shortsighted, Lovejoy believed, for Southerners to try to prevent Negroes from becoming educated. Since they would soon be freed, they must be prepared to accept their new status. Lovejoy was certain that his stand was right, "and sooner than be driven from it," he announced, "we would even—a sad alternative—go over to Abolition ground." If Southerners themselves refused to take the steps that would end slavery by moderate means, then all who desired its eventual disappearance must become abolitionists. Lovejoy understood that point in July, 1834. He was preparing himself for the action he must soon take.[14]

By the spring of 1835 he had clarified his ideas on the ending of slavery and brought them into practical harmony with the position of the American Anti-Slavery Society. At that time an unsuccessful movement was underway to call a convention to revise the state constitution. Lovejoy urged the small antislavery element in Missouri to use the convention as an opportunity either to abolish slavery at once or to end it eventually by restricting the admission of further slaves.[15] The *Missouri Republican* started the discussion in its issue of April 10, 1835, by calling on the voters to work for the "good and glorious cause" of emancipation in Missouri. The scheme it proposed was one of gradual emancipation that would not injure the property rights of slaveowners. This was exactly the kind of moderate plan, initiated

. . . . .

[13] *Ibid.*, July 31, 1834.

[14] *Ibid.*

[15] Lovejoy, *Memoir*, pp. 127-128.

by Southerners themselves, that Lovejoy favored. With characteristic enthusiasm he enlisted the *Observer* in the crusade to end slavery in Missouri, and he offered prayers that an effective leader would appear to direct the movement. "What a glorious opportunity is now offered to such a one," he wrote, "to confer a lasting, an unspeakable benefit upon the citizens of this state . . . and upon the cause of universal humanity!"[16]

Exactly how great he thought the need was he let the public know by publishing on the first page of his newspaper, where no reader would be likely to miss it, a strong article by the Reverend David Nelson emphasizing the religious aspect of slavery. The informing idea of Nelson's essay was that the slave was a human being with a soul, and that his master ought to treat him as a man, not as property. Lovejoy thought the article so important that he wrote a lengthy editorial calling attention to it. Obviously he had found a new major interest, one perfectly in accord with his basic religious and reform impulses and one certain to arouse opposition in Missouri.[17]

Lovejoy insisted at this time that he did not advocate *"immediate and unconditional emancipation,"* but he insisted just as strongly that "something must be done speedily on this all-important subject." "God has not slumbered," he warned, "nor has his Justice been an indifferent spectator of the scene. The groans, and sighs, and tears, and blood of the poor slave have gone up as a memorial before the throne of Heaven. In due time they will descend in awful curses upon this land, unless averted by the speedy repentance of us all." And, he prophesied, "as surely as there is a thunderbolt in Heaven and strength in God's right arm to launch it, so surely will it strike the authors of such cruel oppression."[18]

This was certainly bold language for an editor in a slave state to address to his slaveholding neighbors, and probably few of them missed the implication. In their eyes Lovejoy from that day forward was marked as an abolitionist. Although he still maintained that the label did not fit him, the disclaimer was hardly worth making, for it was perfectly clear that he and the abolitionists shared a common

. . . . .

[16] *Missouri Republican,* April 10 and 21, 1835; Lovejoy, *Memoir,* pp. 124-125.

[17] St. Louis *Observer,* April 16, 1835.

[18] *Ibid.*

spirit. Of course, unlike most other Western abolitionists, Lovejoy had not yet proclaimed slavery to be a sin, but that was a point of minor importance, since nobody but a hairsplitting theologian (which Lovejoy was not) could have explained the difference between sin and an evil so horrendous as to call forth God's avenging thunderbolts.

Two weeks later Lovejoy continued the discussion by presenting his readers with a careful analysis of slavery as he understood it. He rejected completely the Southern argument that slavery had been a good influence on the Negro and on white society. "In every community where it exists," he declared, "it presses like a nightmare on the body politic." Whether considered in its civil, religious, or moral aspects, "it is demonstrably an evil . . . no less the cause of moral corruption to the master than to the slave."

The remedy he proposed—he still insisted upon it—was gradual emancipation. "There is, however, another matter," he continued, "which admits, nay demands a very different mode of treatment. We mean the manner in which the relations subsisting between Christians and their slaves are fulfilled. Here the reform ought to be thorough and immediate. There is no possible plea which can afford excuse for a moment's delay. . . . While on the general subject of Slavery we are decidedly gradual, on this part of it we are as decidedly immediate Abolitionist."[19]

Within another month Lovejoy had begun to warn the people of St. Louis of the danger they faced from slave rebellion, and he suggested they might avoid bloodshed by following the "safe, practicable and expedient" plan of gradual abolition that England had recently inaugurated in the West Indies.[20]

There could be no doubt about it. By the early summer of 1835 Lovejoy had become an abolitionist, perhaps without realizing it, certainly without admitting it. His position was identical with the position of the American Anti-Slavery Society and of many of the Western abolitionists, who, deriving a part of their program from the British example of emancipation in the West Indies, defined their goal as "immediate emancipation, gradually accomplished." They believed, as Lovejoy believed, that the slaves must be freed at once, but held

. . . . .

[19] *Ibid.*, April 30, 1835.

[20] "Letter from the Editor, May 21, 1835," Lovejoy, *Memoir*, p. 131.

under "necessary restraint" until they could be prepared to assume their responsibilities as free men in society.[21]

Lovejoy's protests that he favored *gradual* emancipation did not deceive the slaveholders and other proslavery men in Missouri. He might be able to persuade himself that some fundamental difference could be found between his views and the platform of the American Anti-Slavery Society, but his readers knew better. They could tell an abolitionist when they saw one.

. . . . .

[21] Barnes, *Antislavery Impulse,* pp. 48-49.

Reaction

Chapter VI

At the tag end of summer in 1835 when the crops had been laid by, Elijah Lovejoy rode out from St. Louis through the dry and dusty countryside southwest of the city to take part in a series of revival meetings. At that time of year the fields of the Middle West lie brown from the summer's heat; even the trees seem sometimes to wither at noonday. Men are excitable in that season, their emotions easily aroused. It is a likely time for revivals. It is also a likely time for violence.

The year before, Lovejoy had been ordained as an evangelist by the presbytery of St. Louis.[1] Since then, he had taken part in several camp meetings, using "means" that more conservative churchmen scorned to produce conversions. Nearing the crowded campground, he prepared himself once more for the task of gathering in the harvest of anxious souls.

A frontier revival meeting was an important community affair, usually commanding the services of several of the most eloquent preachers available, and drawing attendance from miles around. Men, women, and children of all ages flocked to such gatherings, some only for sociability and a few to scoff, but most of them to attain the solace of religion and to catch the enthusiasm of the revival preachers. On such occasions as each speaker in his turn arose to address the crowd, the air was filled with fervid sermons about the works of the devil, the dangers of hell, and the saving grace of Christ.

. . . . .

[1] Lovejoy to Elizabeth Lovejoy, June 3, 1834, Wickett-Wiswall Collection.

When Lovejoy's turn came to preach, the members of the congregation prepared themselves for another assault against their worldliness and immorality, another invitation to mend their ways and repent. They were startled by what they heard. For the most part, this dark, well-built young man delivered a conventional revival sermon, but in the same breath in which he condemned whiskey and gambling as snares of the devil, he also condemned slavery. This was fairly new doctrine to that rural audience. Slavery, most people thought, was an inherited institution like any other, one for which the present generation could not be held responsible, and one not to be judged by ordinary moral standards. No doubt it had its bad points, but that it might be a sin as bad as blasphemy or adultery was a disturbing idea that few had considered. Lovejoy did not make slavery the main topic of his sermon, and he chose his language with great care. It was slavery he condemned, not slaveholders. Nonetheless, he said enough to antagonize that minority in his audience whom he was later to characterize as "whip-crackers and cigar-smokers."[2]

Now, more than one frontier preacher in those days saw his meeting broken up by rowdies, and some for less cause than Lovejoy had given. He could not be sure on this occasion that the same thing would not happen to him, for it was easy enough to sense the suspicion, even the hostility, his remarks had created. Most of the people at the camp meeting, however, did not belong to the whip-cracking, cigar-smoking category. They were good farmers, pious and hardworking, who happened to have a personal interest in slavery. They had never considered it a serious problem or thought much about it, one way or the other, and they were not prepared to do so now. Religion was what they had come to the revival for, and religion was what they got. With the meetings ended and the benedictions pronounced, most of them simply went home, spiritually refreshed from their experiences. But two men, fired by more than ordinary proslavery zeal, plotted to teach the disturber a lesson.

They intended to capture Lovejoy as he entered the village of Potosi, where they supposed he planned to spend the night after the

. . . . .

[2] Lovejoy to Absalom Peters, August 19, 1835, AHMS Papers; St. Louis *Observer*, October 1, 1835.

camp meeting. Through the use of tar and feathers, and perhaps other forms of violence, they would help him learn that no man meddles with basic social institutions without paying the consequences. They laid their plans and watched all afternoon and into the night, but Lovejoy failed to arrive. Luckily, a friend some distance from Potosi had given him lodging, so that he did not pass through the village until the next morning. Several hours before he arrived, the pair waiting for him had become impatient and left. When Lovejoy learned of the peril he had so narrowly evaded, he chose to believe that God had delivered him from harm and had spared him to promote His enterprises. A pious man who searched constantly to discover God's will could easily see in the event evidence of himself as God's chosen agent.[3]

Although there had been intimations of violence against Lovejoy before, this was the first real threat to his safety. All summer an elder of the Presbyterian church in St. Louis had warned him that enemies lay in wait, but since nothing untoward had happened, he had dismissed the reports as products of the imagination of a nervous old man. At Potosi he learned that such threats could be real, that danger might lurk in any unexpected place. A man less sure of himself might have faltered at that point and decided to proceed more cautiously. Lovejoy did nothing of the kind. Instead, he determined to continue conducting his affairs as his conscience compelled, and to trust in God for protection. More than ever, as he rode from Potosi toward St. Louis, he thought of himself as an instrument of God working for the renovation of the world. More than ever, he felt himself isolated from an indifferent, perhaps hostile, society that understood neither him nor the purposes of God. But he did not yet know quite how to meet the challenge that had been presented to him. Clearly he would not back down from his antislavery stand. Exactly what the issues were, however, and on what grounds he would oppose those who sought to silence him, he had yet to decide.[4]

As soon as Lovejoy had returned to St. Louis and while he still pondered the implications of his recent narrow escape, the Presbyterian elder who customarily delivered bad tidings visited his office again.

. . . . .

[3] Lovejoy, *Memoir,* p. 161.
[4] *Ibid.*

This time he reported that unknown persons were circulating a handbill encouraging the formation of a mob to wreck the *Observer*'s office. After his experience in Potosi Lovejoy could not easily ignore this new threat. Mobs in St. Louis, he knew, were no longer rare. The year before, an unruly crowd had gathered to burn the governor in effigy; and a few months later a similar group had met one evening to tear down a grog shop of especially evil repute.[5]

Lovejoy knew, too, that powerful elements in St. Louis would be happy to see the *Observer* silenced, that the city newspapers had started an editorial campaign against him and his antislavery views. Recently they had warned businessmen to expect no more Southern emigrants to settle in Missouri if the discussion of slavery continued, and they had hinted that the propagation of abolitionist sentiment might bring about a slave insurrection, the particular horror that was never far from any Southerner's consciousness.

But it was not his newspaper articles alone which antagonized Missourians that fall of 1835. As an agent of the American Bible Society for St. Louis, he had shipped a box of Bibles to the branch society in Jefferson City. When the local officials opened the shipment, they found copies of the *Emancipator,* a newspaper published by the American Anti-Slavery Society, among the packing. Excitement in Jefferson City ran high as news of the incident spread. By including antislavery publications in his Bible shipment, Lovejoy had kindled a spark which, one of his friends in Jefferson City warned, "could be blown up to a blast with but little encouragement." Some of the alarmists were churchmen who deplored the results of any action which might associate the religious reform societies with abolition. Others, more specifically proslavery, were incensed that a resident of St. Louis would himself circulate "foreign" antislavery publications in Missouri.[6]

News of the event led to a series of hostile meetings in St. Louis to protest Lovejoy's antislavery activities and abolitionism in general. At the same time the *Missouri Argus* declared that because of his antislavery stand Lovejoy had forfeited all his rights to courtesy as a news-

. . . . .

[5] St. Louis *Observer,* August 14, 1834.

[6] S. P. Hart to Lovejoy, September 8, 1835, Wickett-Wiswall Collection; St. Louis *Observer,* October 1, November 5, 1835; St. Louis *Commercial Bulletin,* October 21, 1835.

paper editor. No matter what the *Argus* editors may have meant by the remark, readers could easily interpret it as a summons to mob action.[7]

There was obviously no reason at all to minimize the danger. Yet Lovejoy, always the calmest of men, and now, so far as anyone could tell, also the most assured, remained unruffled by the rapidly changing public attitude toward him. He continued his usual work, preparing newspaper copy and now and then delivering evangelistic sermons, apparently unmindful of the growing hostility of the people of St. Louis. Nevertheless, he sent his wife, who was now expecting their first child, to her mother's home at St. Charles, and within a few days he left the city again, perhaps partly in the hope that his continued absence would serve to relieve the developing tension. This time he went into Illinois to attend the commencement exercises at the new college at Jacksonville.[8]

Lovejoy had also attended its commencement in 1834, and now as he neared the little college in its pleasant wooded setting at the outskirts of the Illinois village, he looked forward to renewing the acquaintances he had made before at that frontier outpost of New England culture. Only occasionally in the motley West was it possible for Lovejoy to move in a society congenial to his own ideals. Illinois College provided such an opportunity. Founded half-a-dozen years earlier by a group of zealous young clergymen fresh from the seminaries of New England, the college represented Lovejoy's own standards and values. He could feel completely at home with its faculty, who had come to the West for reasons much like his own. They, too, had felt an overwhelming sense of duty to spread the Gospel and New England ideals into the Mississippi valley.[9]

The president of Illinois College was young Edward Beecher, son of the renowned New England preacher, Lyman Beecher, and brother of Harriet Beecher Stowe, who a few years later would write *Uncle Tom's Cabin.* At almost the same time the elder Beecher had received the appointment as president of Lane Seminary, his son had accepted an

. . . . .

[7] Harrison Anthony Trexler, *Slavery in Missouri, 1804-1865* (Baltimore, Maryland, 1914), p. 116; St. Louis *Missouri Argus,* September 11, 1835.

[8] St. Louis *Observer,* September 21, 1835.

[9] *Ibid.,* October 16, 1834; Charles Henry Rammelkamp, *Illinois College, a Centennial History, 1839-1929* (New Haven, Connecticut, 1928), pp. 10-25.

invitation to become the first president of the infant college in Illinois. In the same spirit that had drawn Lovejoy back to St. Louis in 1833, Beecher had abandoned a promising career in New England to engage, as he said, in "the sublime enterprise of educating and evangelizing [Illinois] so centrally located in the great western valley."[10]

When Lovejoy talked with Beecher and other faculty members during intervals in the commencement proceedings, he found that they too wavered on the point of open adherence to the doctrines of abolition. He gave them as much encouragement as he could, and in due time the religious background all of them shared led the majority to become abolitionists, and the college to become a center of antislavery sentiment. Beecher later wrote that it was in 1835, the year of Lovejoy's second visit to Jacksonville, that he rejected the doctrine of gradual emancipation and accepted immediate emancipation as "philosophical and safe."[11]

The influence of these men was also great on Lovejoy, for martyrs need support. Those who venture to defy the popular will cannot really stand alone. They may possess, as in Lovejoy's case, the assurance of God's favor, but they also need the encouragement of their like-minded fellow men, however few, to sustain them in their testing hours. If Lovejoy felt any doubts about the wisdom of continuing his forthright course in St. Louis, the faculty at Illinois College helped persuade him of his obligation to remain steadfast. By the time he left Jacksonville to begin the journey back home, he had developed renewed assurance, and he had also reinforced his friendship with an important group on whose support he might depend in the troubled times ahead.

He tarried only a few days in St. Louis. By the end of the first week in October, he had left the city again, this time to attend meetings of the presbytery and synod at the towns of Union and Marion in Missouri. In the event that anyone should interpret his repeated absences as a retreat, he published in the *Observer* just before he left a statement of the principles of the American Anti-Slavery Society and announced his agreement with most of them. This was a particularly

. . . . .

[10] Charles Beecher, "The Life of Edward Beecher" (Illinois College Library, Jacksonville), p. 128.

[11] Edward Beecher, *Narrative of Riots at Alton: In Connection with the Death of Rev. Elijah P. Lovejoy* (Alton, 1838), p. 22.

dangerous thing to do at that moment, since only a short time earlier a citizens' meeting in St. Louis had passed resolutions deploring the activities of abolitionists in the state. Now a newspaper in the city ventured to print and circulate the platform of the national organization of abolitionists! There was indeed cause for alarm.[12]

Lovejoy was at Union and thus reasonably safe for the time being. The newspaper office, however, might be damaged if public wrath increased. To prevent this happening, the men who had provided the capital to establish the *Observer* sent a letter to Lovejoy requesting him in the interest of peace "to pass over in silence everything connected with the subject of Slavery. . . ." Important citizens of Missouri had signed the letter: Archibald Gamble, who would later be elected governor of the state; Beverly Allen, a leading lawyer and former United States District Attorney; the Reverend William S. Potts, prominent St. Louis clergyman; Nathan Ranney, successful commission merchant; Dr. G. W. Call, pioneer St. Louis physician; Major Joshua B. Brant, United States Army officer; and several others of similar prestige. In Lovejoy's absence the publishers of the paper, bowing to the wishes of these powerful figures, promised to print nothing more about slavery so long as the editor remained out of the city.[13]

Lovejoy recognized the danger he faced. If men like Archibald Gamble and William Potts would no longer back him, he could not expect to hold off the wrath of the St. Louis mob. For that reason he had a special purpose in attending the church meetings at Union. If he were to survive in Missouri, he must gain the support of respected and influential people. No matter how sincerely he thought of himself as leaning on God alone, no matter how willingly he would sacrifice himself to the cause he believed in, he knew he must show his opponents in St. Louis that responsible men approved his policies. Otherwise the mob would surely attempt to silence him, however theoretically right he might be. For those reasons he took along with him to the presbytery a set of resolutions against slavery. If he could persuade his fellow clergymen to approve them, his opponents would know that in opposing him they opposed also the authority of the Presbyterian church.

. . . . .

[12] St. Louis *Observer,* October 1, 1835.

[13] "To the Rev. E. P. Lovejoy, Editor of the *Observer,*" Lovejoy, *Memoir,* pp. 137-138; St. Louis *Observer,* October 8, 1835.

Realizing that much hung in the balance, Lovejoy appeared before the clergymen assembled in the Presbyterian church at Union to present his resolutions. Almost to a man, the delegates belonged to the liberal wing of Presbyterianism, which accepted the duty of the church to promote social reform. Already they were convinced that the church should officially condemn slavery. When the vote on Lovejoy's resolutions was taken, every member of the presbytery voted for them. It was a personal triumph for Lovejoy. As the clergymen adjourned to join the meeting of the synod farther north at Marion, he felt encouraged by the support the antislavery cause had received.[14]

He thought there was good reason to expect this success to be repeated at Marion, for Marion County was a center of general reform activity. More copies of the *Observer* circulated in Marion than any place except St. Louis itself, and among the members of the synod were several avowedly abolitionist professors from Marion College, the school David Nelson had recently established.[15] The composition of this body, however, differed significantly from the presbytery at Union. It included a large number of representatives from parts of the state where new-school ideas had hardly penetrated. In particular, the elders—the lay officials of the church—tended to be decidedly more conservative on social issues than the ordained clergy, and they could not so easily understand the moral and religious implications of slavery.

When Lovejoy had presented his antislavery resolutions for adoption, an elder from St. Louis arose to argue against them. The resolutions were filled with hidden danger, he warned. However appealing it might be to the humanitarian impulses of the clergy to go on record as opposing slavery, they must realize that the Presbyterian church in Missouri would certainly be torn by faction and perhaps destroyed if it took a stand sympathetic with abolitionist doctrine. In any event, its reform societies would suffer should they become tinged with abolitionism. Those practical considerations naturally seemed very important to the dark-coated elders and to some of the clergy as well. When the vote was taken, they rejected Lovejoy's resolutions.[16]

. . . .

[14] Lovejoy, *Memoir,* p. 161.
[15] Ephraim Strong to Absalom Peters, December 24, 1836, AHMS Papers.
[16] Lovejoy, *Memoir,* pp. 161-162.

Although the synod agreed to condemn slavery as a great evil which ought to be ended, it also criticized "the unjustifiable course pursued by the abolitionists on the subject of domestic slavery." Such an official rebuke could hardly go unnoticed in St. Louis, where it contributed to the growing fear of the results of abolitionism. Before the synod adjourned, mob violence erupted in the city. With every passing day, citizens had become more concerned about the activities of the abolitionists who they thought were operating in the city. By the middle of October, while the synod and presbytery were meeting, the concern approached hysteria as the public became convinced that abolitionists were plotting to encourage insurrection among the colored population. Slaveowners in the city thought they sensed a new spirit of insubordination among their "property." Ordinary citizens eyed the free Negroes they met with fear, and it was against the freedmen that much of the hostility focused. The *Missouri Republican*'s ominous warning that "the long nights are again approaching" when the Negroes in the city might rise against the whites, frightened readers who were already worried about the possibility of a slave revolt.[17]

At that moment two men from Illinois named Fuller and Bridges helped several slaves owned in St. Louis to escape across the river. Angry men from St. Louis pursued both the slaves and their benefactors into Illinois and brought them back to the city. There they were met by a mob of sixty enraged citizens, who whipped Fuller and Bridges and threatened to lynch them. Not content with this, the mob looked about for some other object upon which to vent their wrath. Though the proprietors of the *Observer* had kept their promise to print no more antislavery articles while Lovejoy remained out of the city, some of the mob threatened to wreck the newspaper office anyway. Only the proprietors' public announcement that they were prepared to use force to defend their property saved the *Observer* from destruction.[18]

On October 24, 1835, the popular uproar achieved formal organization when a mass meeting convened to decide on further action. Al-

. . . . .

[17] *Missouri Republican,* October 20, 1835.

[18] Benjamin Merkel, *The Antislavery Controversy in Missouri, 1819-1865* (St. Louis, Missouri, 1942), p. 8; Lovejoy, *Memoir,* pp. 136-137; *Missouri Republican,* October 22, 1835; St. Louis *Observer,* October 22, 1835.

though the assembly was entirely extralegal, it possessed all the prestige that authority could possibly give it. Its meeting place was the courthouse, many of the city's most respected citizens attended, and former mayor William Carr Lane presided. At their second session held a week later the citizens got around to the work they had met to accomplish. The bulk of their resolutions concerned the presence in the city of free Negroes who had moved to Missouri contrary to state law. This group, the meeting charged, constituted a grave danger to social stability and should be expelled. The citizens then passed resolutions condemning abolitionist doctrine and activity, and, although Lovejoy and the *Observer* were not mentioned by name, it was obviously they who were held largely responsible for whatever abolitionist influence existed in the city. The committee that drew up those resolutions was composed of intelligent and educated men who knew that in openly opposing the course of editors like Lovejoy they might be accused of trifling with the constitutional rights of free speech and a free press. Accordingly, they thought it wise to justify their action on the ground that the activities of the abolitionists were "seditious, and calculated to incite insurrection and anarchy, and ultimately, a disseverment of our prosperous Union." In such an emergency, they said, ordinary constitutional guarantees could not apply.

The rest of the committee's resolutions were designed to appeal to the prejudices of the more simple-minded. "Infatuated Abolitionists," they warned, promoted the "preposterous and impudent doctrine" of amalgamation—the intermarriage of whites and Negroes. The resolutions concluded on a religious note by asserting that slavery had been practiced by the prophets of Israel and was in every respect sanctioned by the Bible.

All this served to express the sentiment of the meeting, but that had not been the sole purpose for holding it. The citizens had been called together to take positive action against free Negroes and abolitionists—if the government could not control them, the people must do so. They voted to form a committee of vigilance in each ward of the city and in each township in the county. Their activities would be coordinated by a committee of correspondence to which the important politician Thomas Hart Benton was appointed. These little groups would make a list of all free Negroes living in the area, with the aim of driving out those not born in Missouri or those not closely related to locally owned slaves. They would also ferret out persons suspected of being abolitionists and report to the authorities anyone suspected of preaching or publishing abolitionist doctrine. Then, if government officials failed to suppress such persons, another mass meeting would be called to decide how to deal with the situation. Thus the St. Louis meeting established in every community extralegal machinery by which neighbor was encouraged to spy against neighbor and act as informer against the suspect. The people of St. Louis had proclaimed that they did not trust their government and planned to act independently of it.[19]

Since Lovejoy was then engaged in the deliberations at Marion, he had of course not been party to any of these ominous proceedings. Not until the synod was about to adjourn did news reach Marion about the flogging of Fuller and Bridges at St. Louis. Great excitement swept through the assembled clergy as they heard accounts of the violence. Judging from the exaggerated reports that came from St. Louis, they thought it altogether unlikely that an abolitionist could hope to remain alive within the city. Most of the clergymen at the synod faced no personal problem from the situation, for they were not popularly considered abolitionists, but one of their number was. As the delegates talked in hushed tones about the shocking events in St. Louis, their eyes turned toward Lovejoy, who must now go home to resume the editorship of his newspaper in a city swept by antiabolitionist hysteria.[20]

. . . . .

[19] St. Louis *Commercial Bulletin,* October 29, 1835; *Missouri Republican,* October 27, November 7, 1835; St. Louis *Observer,* November 5, 1835.

[20] Lovejoy, *Memoir,* p. 162.

Determined in the Cause

Chapter VII

Lovejoy set out for home with the foreknowledge that entrance into St. Louis might make real the violence he had escaped at Potosi. For seventy miles he traveled through the autumn-colored countryside with one of his colleagues from the synod, talking with him about the problem as they jogged along the crude road that led toward St. Louis. Practically all the members of the synod had advised him not to return to the city. As they shook his hand to bid him farewell, they appealed to him for the sake of his wife and unborn child to take no chances with his personal safety. Lovejoy was moved by such considerations, and yet he knew too that long ago he had dedicated his life to a cause he believed greater than earthly security. Here for the first time he must decide whether he was prepared to make the sacrifice such dedication might require.[1]

The mental conflict and the strain of many weeks of work and travel had left him exhausted. By the time he arrived at St. Charles, where Celia, his wife, was staying, he had become so ill that he could go no farther. For three days he remained in that quiet river town, struggling with his conscience, discussing the problem with his wife and praying for divine guidance to help him reconcile his responsibilities to his family with his responsibilities to God. At last he made up his mind—whatever the danger, he must return to St. Louis. He would go back and denounce mob rule and defend the freedom of the press. . . . . .

[1] Lovejoy, *Memoir*, p. 162.

Celia concurred in his decision, and he left her, ready to accept whatever fate might be his.[2]

He entered the city quietly and was noticed by only a few. The friends he met warned him to stay out of the streets. Feeling against him remained intense, they reported, and no one could predict the lengths to which his enemies would go to oppose him. Only a scattering of people in the entire city, he realized, were willing to support him against the hostility of the populace. He was alone. For a moment, as he realized his peril, an awful fear possessed him; but then he recalled the dozens of fellow clergymen in Illinois and elsewhere who believed as he did and who looked to him to maintain the faith. As the conviction grew within him that God offered him solace and aid in the struggle for what he believed right, his resolution became unshakeable. He would live by faith alone. Opposition was forcing Lovejoy to assume the role of a martyr. Having found the path of duty, he resolved that not all the fury of men or devils should drive him from it. "I think I could have gone to the stake and not a nerve have trembled, nor a lip quivered," he later told his brother.[3]

Thus strengthened, Lovejoy set himself to preparing an exposition of the issues involved in the controversy. He soon published in the *Observer* an eloquent address to the people of St. Louis, designed, he said, to maintain his rights "as a republican citizen, free-born of these United States, and to defend fearlessly, the cause of TRUTH AND RIGHTEOUSNESS." But he added to his appeal for civil rights a note of impassioned bigotry. Hostility to the *Observer* did not result from its antislavery position, he declared. "The real origin of the cry 'Down with the *Observer*' is to be looked for in its opposition to Popery. The fire that is now blazing and crackling through this city, was kindled on Popish altars and has been assiduously blowed up by Jesuit breath."[4]

In this statement Lovejoy was mistaken. Some of his most determined opponents were Roman Catholics, and no doubt his religious stand had contributed to the disrepute in which he was held. Yet there is no reason to believe that opposition to him would not have devel-

. . . . .

[2] *Ibid.*

[3] *Ibid.*, p. 163.

[4] "To My Fellow Citizens," St. Louis *Observer*, November 5, 1835.

oped exactly as it did had he never mentioned the Catholic church. Editors of antislavery newspapers encountered opposition nearly everywhere in 1835. The people of the slave state of Missouri would have shown forbearance indeed had they failed to protest so extreme an antislavery stand as Lovejoy had taken.

Having disposed of this issue, at least to his own satisfaction, he then addressed himself to the special grievance many had against him—that he had sent copies of the *Emancipator* to Jefferson City. This provided him with the occasion for presenting his first well-developed statement of his views on the freedom of the press. Although he admitted that exchange copies of abolitionist newspapers were in his office, he denied that he had sent any of them to Jefferson City, except inadvertently as part of the packing in a crate of Bibles. On the other hand, he defended his right "to send ten thousand of them," if he chose, to as many citizens. It was not the privilege of a mob, he insisted, to decide whether he could do so or not; nor was it the right of a mob to dictate what he could print in his newspaper. Slavery, he repeated, was a wicked institution, and in discussing it, he only exercised rights guaranteed by the constitution of the United States and the constitution of Missouri. "I cannot surrender my principles," he asserted, "though the whole world besides should vote them down—I can make no compromise between truth and error, even though my life be the alternative." Lovejoy understood, if others did not, that the principle of freedom of the press was at stake. The issue was not whether slavery was right or wrong or whether the Catholic church was as bad as he said it was, but whether he possessed the right to discuss these subjects in the public press.[5]

To those people in St. Louis who hoped their opposition would force him to decide to leave the city and move to a free state, Lovejoy offered a solemn promise. He would remain where he was, continue to print whatever his conscience directed, and abide the consequences. "The path of duty lies plain before me," he declared, "and I must walk therein, even though it lead to . . . the stake."[6]

He had made his position clear; the initiative was now left to the

. . . . .

[5] *Ibid.*

[6] *Ibid.*; Lovejoy to his brother, November 2 and 10, 1835, Lovejoy, *Memoir,* pp. 155-158.

populace. He could do little but wait. Although he certainly knew that violence might overwhelm him at any moment, there is no reason to suppose that he did not share, even in that peril, his mother's confidence in his perfect security. "He will be safe," she wrote, "though the earth be removed out of its place and the mountains carried into the midst of the sea."[7]

For two days, however, the issue remained in doubt. No one, except perhaps the consecrated, could be sure whether Lovejoy's eloquent plea would calm the popular wrath or whether it would lead to new outbreaks of violence. But eventually the atmosphere cleared. Lovejoy's appeal for the support of civil rights had succeeded. The *Missouri Republican* asserted that no mob action had ever been planned against Lovejoy. The Catholic publication, *The Shepherd of the Valley,* categorically denied the existence of any Catholic agitation against the *Observer* and pleaded innocent to charges that it was intolerant of Protestants.[8] Men in St. Louis who had never before been friendly with Lovejoy, men who were not personally concerned with the slavery controversy at all, arose to defend his civil rights. Letters poured into the *Observer*'s office from many quarters in Missouri and Illinois bearing congratulations for the stand he had taken. Edward Beecher, president of Illinois College, interrupted his observance of the Sabbath to write Lovejoy a letter endorsing the principles he had adopted and approving the manner in which he had defended them "as truly in accordance with the meekness and yet courage demanded in a soldier of the cross, in fighting the battles of the Lord." Many prominent men in St. Louis who had been swept along by the wave of popular indignation now offered to support Lovejoy's right to discuss slavery, even though they did not personally share his antislavery views. Thus, hostile citizens, left without either leadership or support, offered no more opposition.[9]

The owners of the *Observer,* however, reacted differently. When they learned that Lovejoy intended to continue printing antislavery

. . . . .

[7] Elizabeth Lovejoy to Owen Lovejoy, November 30, 1835, Owen Lovejoy Papers.

[8] *Shepherd of the Valley,* November 7 and 21, 1835, cited in "Elijah P. Lovejoy as an Anti-Catholic," p. 178.

[9] *Missouri Republican,* November 7, 1835; Lovejoy, *Memoir,* p. 164; Beecher to Lovejoy, December 20, 1835, Wickett-Wiswall Collection.

material and budge not an inch from his position, they came to him immediately and requested him to retire as editor. Although the terms of their agreement were such that they could not legally force him to give up his position, he knew that he could not continue his editorship without their friendly support. He gave up in defeat, turned his office over to the proprietors, and concluded that his work in St. Louis was finished. He had fought a good fight, but he had lost, and though the disappointment was great, there was, after all, no disgrace in it.[10]

The proprietors then transferred the property to the holder of the mortgage, a wealthy St. Louis moneylender, expecting him to sell it at public auction. Instead, the mortgagee experienced a change of heart. Visiting Lovejoy, he found him in the office of the *Observer,* packing his belongings and surrounded by a confusion of press and paper and ink. He had decided not to sell the newspaper after all, he announced. He thought it should continue; he would return the entire property to Lovejoy.

Nothing could have been more welcome to Lovejoy, of course, or more unexpected. His benefactor attached one condition to the offer, however. Since public excitement remained so fevered in St. Louis that the *Observer* for practical reasons could probably no longer safely be published there, Lovejoy must move the enterprise to Alton, the thriving river town across the border in the free state of Illinois. Even though Lovejoy knew that such an arrangement would generally be interpreted as a retreat by him and a victory for the mob, he could see no alternative. After all, the paper had been saved as by a miracle, and he must accept the condition of its salvation. So he left the next day for Alton to make plans to establish the *Observer* there.[11]

While he was in Alton arranging to rent an office and attempting to gauge the state of public opinion in that city, an unexpected letter arrived from St. Louis. The holder of the mortgage and others had changed their minds again. They now believed that yielding to public pressure in any respect was the wrong thing to do. It would be better, they had decided, to keep the paper in Missouri. Since that had al-

. . . . .

[10] Lovejoy, *Memoir,* pp. 164-165; Lovejoy to Archibald Gamble, November 27, 1835, Autograph Collection of Simon Gratz (Historical Society of Pennsylvania, Philadelphia).

[11] Lovejoy, *Memoir,* p. 165.

ways been Lovejoy's opinion, he welcomed their invitation to return to St. Louis.[12]

For the present, at least, many of the leaders of public opinion in St. Louis were ashamed of their recent conduct. Lovejoy's firm stand for freedom of speeech and freedom of the press had won their respect and thus produced a momentary halt in the violence. But Lovejoy was not optimistic. Suppose he continued to print whatever his conscience directed. Could he then expect the toleration of the multitude? Although the air had temporarily cleared, he held no illusions about his security in the city. "The time is soon coming," he predicted, "when we must all be tried by fire."[13]

Lovejoy was not mistaken. Powerful agencies in St. Louis, unreconciled to his return, persisted in their agitation against him. The *Missouri Argus* published letters reminding its readers that the *Observer* was not really an official organ of the Presbyterian church, which was true; and a prominent Presbyterian, writing in the *Missouri Republican,* informed Lovejoy that his policy did not "meet the wishes of many of your brethren," and promoted "neither the harmony nor respectability of the Presbyterian Church in Missouri." Early in December another public mass meeting, much smaller than those held in November, condemned efforts to educate Negroes and resolved to demand that Lovejoy cease publishing antislavery articles.[14]

An abolitionist could no longer expect to speak freely in the South without experiencing retaliation. As antislavery agitation throughout the North increased, it produced a corresponding reaction in the slave states. By 1835 slaveholders were afraid—afraid that their slave property would be taken away from them, afraid that abolitionists would stir up a slave rebellion. Rumors circulated in November, 1835, that slaves in nearby Kentucky had plotted an insurrection, and even in Illinois, a free state, citizens held mass meetings to make plans for the protection of the white population in the event the outbreak occurred. It was hardly strange, then, that the citizens of St. Louis regarded Lovejoy and his newspaper with apprehension.[15]

. . . . .

[12] *Ibid.*

[13] Lovejoy to Absalom Peters, December 31, 1835, AHMS Papers.

[14] *Missouri Argus,* November 27, December 11, 1835; *Missouri Republican,* November 24, December 8, 1835.

[15] Alton *Spectator,* December 3, 1835.

Because of the rapidly changing attitude toward antislavery ideas, there seemed no hope that Lovejoy could long propagate his views in the slaveholding city of St. Louis. With the increasing hostility, the *Observer*'s subscriptions fell off to the point that Lovejoy made no money at all from his labor on the newspaper, and for the support of his family he had to depend almost entirely on the $200 a year paid him by the American Home Missionary Society. "My trials are exceedingly great," he admitted, "and nothing but the stern convictions of duty hinder me from leaving my present post."[16]

Every week it became clearer that if the *Observer* were to have any future that future must be in Illinois. Although the paper's support remained slight and tenuous in St. Louis, it was otherwise in Illinois. There its circulation continued to grow as increasing numbers of prominent figures in the Presbyterian and Congregational churches came to its aid.[17]

Meanwhile, under the stress of continued opposition, Lovejoy's antislavery views became more extreme. In the House of Representatives congressmen had adopted a "gag rule" to prevent the reading of antislavery petitions on the floor of Congress. Lovejoy was indignant at what he considered a violation of the right of citizens to petition their lawmaking body. He doubted that the majority of Americans understood the significance of this infringement on their rights. He wanted to express his opinions on the subject through a medium other than the *Observer,* a place where they would be read and not dismissed immediately simply because he happened to be their author. For that reason he made secret arrangements with the editor of the Alton *Telegraph,* in whose office his brother John now worked, to publish a series of articles in defense of the right of citizens to petition Congress. Thus people in Illinois, and probably many in Missouri too, read Lovejoy's essays in the *Telegraph,* never suspecting that they came from the pen of a controversial abolitionist.[18]

The right to petition, Lovejoy told the readers of the *Telegraph,* was in accordance with natural law, which was superior to any human legislation. The Constitution had not created the right of the

. . . . .

[16] Lovejoy to Absalom Peters, December 1, 1835, February 22, 1836, AHMS Papers.
[17] St. Louis *Observer,* October 1, 1835, January 7, 1836.
[18] John Lovejoy to Owen Lovejoy, March 27, 1836, Owen Lovejoy Papers.

people to petition; it had only recognized a pre-existing right. "The right existed before the Constitution was formed," he concluded, "and would have been as perfect as it now is, had that instrument been wholly silent on the subject."[19] Lovejoy had thus adopted the higher law doctrine, the final recourse of revolutionists. What if the population raged, what if statutes and constitutions offered no support—a higher law than that made by man determined correct policy. Lovejoy in that manner early placed himself in the long line of rebels who have appealed to Heaven—or nature—for their rights when all earth has stood against them.

At the same time these essays appeared, Lovejoy printed his most extreme article against slavery. By February, 1836, he had gone as far as it was possible to go in antislavery opinion. "Our creed is that slavery is a *sin*—now, heretofore, hereafter, and forever, a sin," he announced. "Consequently it follows that whoever has participated, or does now participate, in that sin, ought to repent without a moment's delay." If there had been any doubt before that Lovejoy was an abolitionist, none could now remain. Because he believed that the slaves, when freed, should be held in trust until they could be trained for citizenship, he continued to insist in public that the term "abolitionist" did not fit him; yet in private correspondence he admitted to being an "abolitionist of the first water." Although "emancipation cannot be effected in a minute," he said, good men were nonetheless obliged "to *begin* the work of abolition immediately, and to carry it on *in good faith,* as fast as it can be done." His position thus was the same as that of most of the other Western abolitionists, who also did not advocate the immediate and unconditional freeing of all slaves. Lovejoy clearly belonged to their brotherhood—a man's refusal to wear a label by no means lessens his right to wear it.[20]

It is not likely that he would have gone so far in this matter had his opponents not driven him to an extreme position. Like many other abolitionists, he had originally been a colonizationist and a believer in gradual emancipation, fondly hoping that all reformers

. . . . .

[19] Alton *Telegraph,* February 17 and 24, March 2, 1836.

[20] St. Louis *Observer,* February 11, 1836; Lovejoy to Edwin F. Hatfield, January 21, 1836 (Massachusetts Historical Society, Boston).

could unite to deal in peace and harmony with the slavery problem as they had dealt with other such problems. Such cooperation had proved impossible, however, and events had convinced him that those persons who favored a moderate course toward slavery were, either by intent or in spite of their wishes, actually helping to perpetuate it. Moreover, he had learned that slaveowners evinced no intention of ever ending slavery themselves, for even moderate criticism aroused their violent protests. Since Southerners could not be expected to take antislavery action and since all moderate antislavery programs had proved ineffective, only the abolitionist program appeared to hold any hope of success. Because no middle ground remained, Lovejoy adopted the abolitionist position.[21]

But for two months in the late winter and early spring of 1836 he printed very little on the subject. He had accomplished at least something toward the defense of civil rights simply by remaining in St. Louis; and, having made his position on slavery clear, he saw no need to say more about it at the moment. Thus during the spring he published his newspaper, undisturbed by the citizens of St. Louis. In contrast to the preceding autumn this was a time of calm for the Lovejoy family and even of some little prosperity.

Elijah and Celia Lovejoy's first child was born in March. They named him Edward Payson after the famous Maine Congregational divine, whose sermons were widely read at the time. Two months later they and their infant son traveled to Pittsburgh to attend the meeting of the general assembly of the Presbyterian church. Since early winter they had been planning the trip. Celia had never been East before; the change, Elijah thought, would be good for her after the many troubles of the preceding year. He would be going officially as a delegate from the St. Louis presbytery, of which he had recently been elected moderator. But his special reason for wanting to be in Pittsburgh was to aid in the defense of the Reverend Albert Barnes, who had helped him two years before to get his first ministerial appointment at Newport, Rhode Island.[22]

Technically, the general assembly was trying Barnes on the charge

. . . . .

[21] Lovejoy had forecast that this would happen, St. Louis *Observer*, July 31, 1834.

[22] Lovejoy to Absalom Peters, December 18, 1835, AHMS Papers; St. Louis *Observer*, April 28, 1836.

of heresy—he had emphasized man's ability for self-direction—but in a sense his trial symbolized the struggle for power within the Presbyterian church between the conservative theologians and those liberals, with whom Barnes was identified, who accepted Finney's "new measures," minimized the Calvinistic doctrine of predestination, and urged church participation in such reforms as abolition. Lovejoy, of course, belonged with the latter group and wanted to support them when they defended Barnes. At Pittsburgh in 1836 the liberals succeeded in gathering enough votes to acquit Barnes, although they could not carry the general assembly on all issues.[23]

A meeting of the general assembly was of more than ordinary significance to the nation, for it brought together the greatest men in Presbyterianism from all parts of the United States to discuss every sort of issue important to the church. In addition to their importance as legislative bodies, the meetings also provided an opportunity for leaders of opinion to exchange ideas, share experiences, and develop a solidarity of opinion useful in carrying out the church's program of religion and reform.

Lovejoy met with his fellow clergymen at Pittsburgh, discussed his problems with them, and learned at first hand about religious and political affairs in other sections of the nation. They told him that the accounts he had read in the newspapers concerning proslavery mobs were not exaggerated. It was true, they reported, that throughout the North antislavery editors and speakers encountered violent opposition wherever they appeared, that an antislavery orator might expect to have to face a mob armed with stones and brickbats, that an antislavery editor might be called upon to watch his printing press battered into pieces. The antislavery movement in 1836 was undergoing a critical test that would decide whether public pressure could stifle free discussion everywhere in the nation. Lovejoy knew, even before he went to Pittsburgh, that he played a key part in that test.

The general assembly, he found, could not agree on the subject of slavery. The flood of memorials and petitions that poured in upon the assembly requesting it to take an official stand on the matter had been referred to a committee for study and recommendation. Those dele-

. . . . .

[23] Cole, *Social Ideas,* p. 44.

gates who agreed with Lovejoy that the Presbyterian church should throw its authority behind the antislavery cause awaited the presentation of the report with extraordinary interest, for the support of the church would immeasurably aid in promoting the antislavery movement. But the reading of the report brought them disappointment, although hardly surprise. Lovejoy, as he heard the committee's recommendations, must have been reminded of the fate his own antislavery resolutions had met at the Marion synod the preceding October.

The slavery question, reported the committee, had created unusual diversity of opinion and intensity of feeling within the nation. Since any action the assembly might take would only "distract and divide" the church, the committee advised the assembly to drop the whole matter. The committee's recommendation to evade the issue may have been a work of statesmanship, but it was hardly in accord with the consciences of Lovejoy and the many other antislavery men present at Pittsburgh.[24]

Acting for them, the Reverend James H. Dickey, a prominent Ohio abolitionist, presented a strong counterreport urging the church to come forth as the defender of civil rights. Lovejoy heard him remind the assembly that since the sixteenth century, Presbyterians had stood among the foremost advocates of civil and religious liberty. Now in 1836, he said, their reluctance to speak out in defense of those liberties served to strengthen slavery in the South and to weaken human rights everywhere. Efforts to stifle the discussion of slavery, Dickey warned his fellow delegates, conflicted with basic American ideals of liberty, and for the Presbyterian clergy to be silent on the subject was to be "recreant to the cause of truth and mercy, false to their brethren" and to God. Let the church declare its "unwavering and undiminished attachment" to the principles of human rights expressed in the Declaration of Independence, Dickey urged.[25]

Hearing these words, Lovejoy could examine his own conscience and conclude that he had proved neither recreant nor false. Whatever the church might decide to do, Lovejoy was prepared to reaffirm his

. . . . .

[24] *Minutes of the General Assembly of the Presbyterian Church in the United States of America, 1836* (Philadelphia, Pennsylvania, 1836), pp. 247-248.

[25] *Ibid.*, pp. 248-250.

undiminished attachment to the principles of the Declaration of Independence and of the Christian faith as he understood them.

Although Dickey had prepared his report with care and delivered it with eloquence, he failed to persuade the majority of the delegates, who were intent on preserving the institutional unity of the church. On June 7 a resolution to postpone the subject indefinitely carried by a vote of 154 to 87. Lovejoy then joined twenty-seven other members of the assembly to present a formal protest against the entire procedure. The issue, however, had been disposed of, although for only a little while. A year later slavery would be an important factor in bringing about the expulsion of certain synods and the eventual division of the church into its new-school and old-school wings.[26]

The proceedings in the assembly reflected the fact that by 1836 efforts to defend such traditional American rights as freedom of speech, freedom of the press, freedom of the mails, and the right of petition had merged with the antislavery movement.[27] Abolitionists, it appeared, protested against the encroachment on the civil rights not only of Negroes held as slaves but of free white men as well. As Lovejoy left the meetings, he could better relate his own experiences to events in other parts of the nation and be strengthened in his conviction that his conduct in Missouri during the preceding months had been proper, a major part of a vital nationwide cause.

The Lovejoy family returned to Missouri by way of the Great Lakes, stopping briefly in Detroit and Chicago. On their way across Illinois early in July, they visited for four days in Peoria at the home of the Reverend Jeremiah Porter, one of Elijah's ministerial colleagues and a fellow graduate of Princeton Theological Seminary. By the time Lovejoy arrived in Peoria, he had already received news of further disturbing developments in St. Louis that would make his remaining in that city dangerous if not impossible. He and Celia had thought much about the problem. Now, in the intimacy of Porter's home, Lovejoy confided to his host that he feared slaveholders would soon drive him from St. Louis. If the wrath of the populace fell upon him,

. . . . .

[26] *Ibid.*, pp. 272-273.

[27] Russell B. Nye, *Fettered Freedom: Civil Liberties and the Slavery Controversy, 1830-1860* (East Lansing, Michigan, 1949), pp. 121, 137-138.

he said, he intended to take refuge in Alton, Illinois. "It is deplorable," reflected Porter, who would himself soon join the abolitionists, "that St. Louis will banish from its bounds a religious Editor. But this is one of the fruits of Slavery & Popery. Where Slavery exists piety must be banished."[28]

As Elijah and Celia Lovejoy boarded the steamboat that carried them away from Peoria, they enjoyed the last brief interlude of tranquillity that would ever be given them. They already knew before they reached St. Louis that the fury of the Missouri mob had struck at last. While the assembly in Pittsburgh had been debating the issue of slavery and civil rights, the *Observer*'s press in St. Louis had been damaged. And in a separate outbreak a mob had driven the Reverend David Nelson out of the state because of his antislavery opinions.

. . . . .

[28] Journals of Jeremiah Porter, July 3 and 7, August 11, 1836 (Chicago Historical Society).

Violence in Missouri

Chapter VIII

During the evening of April 28, 1836, not long before the Lovejoy family departed for Pittsburgh, a mob lynched a Negro in St. Louis. The circumstances from which the violence developed were not unusual. Two boatmen recently ashore after a long river trip fell into a noisy argument and began fighting on the steamboat landing. As they rolled and wrestled on the ground, deputy sheriff George Hammond and deputy constable William Mull appeared and arrested them for disturbing the peace of that spring afternoon.

While the officers were performing their duty, Francis J. McIntosh, a Negro cook from the steamboat *Flora,* recently docked from Pittsburgh, rushed up and attacked them, apparently hoping to free his quarrelsome acquaintances. In the confusion the two boatmen jerked themselves free and disappeared among the boxed goods along the wharf. McIntosh, however, was not so lucky. The officers arrested him for interfering with their duties and took him before a nearby justice of the peace, who ordered him sent to jail to await trial.

As the officers led McIntosh down the street, he asked them what his punishment would be. He could hardly receive less than twenty-five or thirty lashes at the whipping post, they told him. With that, McIntosh broke loose, drew a long knife that he had kept concealed, and brandishing it about, severely wounded Mull and severed Hammond's jugular vein.[1]

. . . . .

[1] St. Louis *Observer,* May 5, 1836; John Devoy, *A History of the City of St. Louis and Vicinity, from the Earliest Times to the Present* (St. Louis, Missouri, 1898), pp.

The cries of the wounded men quickly brought help, and McIntosh was easily captured and thrown in the jail. Meanwhile a large crowd gathered to stare at the lifeless body of Hammond weltering in blood. The horror of the event seemed to demand immediate action. "Hang him," someone cried. "Burn him," came another voice. Quickly transformed into a vengeful mob, the spectators surged toward the jail. There they were met by the sheriff, who made a gesture to halt them; but fearful for the safety of his family, which had living quarters in the same building that housed the jail, he resisted only feebly.

While the mob prepared to break down the jail doors, someone with a strong, clear voice got their attention. McIntosh was guilty of murder, he began, and should surely be hanged. All could agree on that. But, he pleaded, let the courts make the decision. Let everything be done in a constitutional, legal fashion. The mob, however, was relentless. It wanted revenge, and it wanted it now, before the sun had set on Hammond's dead body.

After breaking down the jail doors, they dragged McIntosh out of his cell and carried him to a locust tree not many blocks away. While he prayed and sang hymns, they chained him to the trunk of the tree, piled old boards around him, and kindled a fire. The crowd watched while the flames leaped high around the man; they listened while he begged someone to shoot him; they waited until he had burned to death; and then they went home.

The next day about noon Lovejoy walked to the scene of the burning and looked upon the blackened and mutilated trunk of McIntosh, still bound to the locust tree. Boys had stoned the body; the head was gone. In revulsion and in pity, Lovejoy turned away. This horrible scene, he concluded, had resulted from uncontrolled popular fury and the rejection of the principles of law and civilized justice. He knew that there was a difference only in degree but not in kind between the action of this mob and of those persons who had lately tried to silence him. Struck by the burden of guilt he and all other men must bear for the fiery rites of the evening before, he prayed that he too might die.[2]

42-44; Alton *Telegraph*, May 4, 1836; John Lovejoy to Elizabeth Lovejoy, April 30, 1836, Wickett-Wiswall Collection.

[2] St. Louis *Observer*, May 5, 1836.

Leaving the site of the lynching, Lovejoy returned home and wrote an impassioned account of what had happened and its meaning. Such events, he wanted his readers to understand, could produce only the most terrible consequences, for mob action of the kind then becoming increasingly common in all parts of the country would eventually destroy the very foundation of civilized society.[3]

Shortly after his article had appeared under the title "Awful Murder and Savage Barbarity," the Lovejoy family left for Pittsburgh and tried to put the event out of their minds. Some people in St. Louis, he knew, blamed him for everything that had happened. Even his young brother John thought the abolitionists were in some way responsible for the atrocity. Lovejoy's newspaper should be silenced, some said, because his antislavery articles tended to encourage Negroes to acts of violence. Didn't the praying and the hymn singing of McIntosh prove that he had been influenced by abolitionists? In spite of the increasing public hostility no attack was made against the newspaper office at that time, although a few weeks later Judge Luke E. Lawless of St. Louis claimed that only his timely intervention had prevented an angry mob from marching to wreck the building.[4]

In May, while Lovejoy was in Pittsburgh, some of the participants in the lynch mob were brought before a grand jury in Judge Lawless' court for indictment. The able, erratic Irish-born judge, who had no sympathy for the cause of abolition, used the occasion to deliver from the bench a splenetic lecture on the evils and dire effects of abolitionist propaganda. He identified the *Observer* with the most extreme kind of abolitionism and contrived to blame Lovejoy, whom he later termed a "sanctimonious enthusiast," for inciting McIntosh to violence.[5]

Judge Lawless has frequently been severely criticized for the position he took during the St. Louis disturbances, and by twentieth-century standards he was wrong; yet his error should not be allowed to obscure the shrewd insights he revealed about the abolitionists. They appeared

. . . . .

[3] *Ibid.*

[4] John Lovejoy to Elizabeth Lovejoy, April 30, 1836, Wickett-Wiswall Collection; *Missouri Republican,* May 26, 1836.

[5] *Missouri Republican,* May 26, 1836; W. V. N. Bay, *Reminiscences of the Bench and Bar of Missouri* (St. Louis, Missouri, 1878), pp. 440-447; *Missouri Argus,* July 1, 1836.

to him, so he told the grand jury, "to labor under a sort of religious hallucination—a monomania—for which it would perhaps be inconsistent with sound reasoning to hold them morally responsible. . . . They seem to consider themselves as special agents . . . in fact, of Divine Providence. They seem to have their eyes fixed on some mystic vision—some Zion, as they term it, within whose holy walls they would impound us all, or condemn us to perish on the outside. But, although all this may be very sincere, is it the less pernicious? Are we to be victims of those sanctimonious madmen?"

Judge Lawless was correct when he suggested that the leading abolitionists, including Lovejoy, were religious zealots convinced that they alone could read God's will, and it is true, too, that they were bent on imposing their revolutionary ideas upon all Americans. But Lawless erred in other of his charges. The judge thought the particular means by which these "madmen" would claim their victims was through a slave rebellion, which, he stated, their publications were designed to encourage. This was not true. Very few of the abolitionists advocated a slave uprising, and Lovejoy was not one of them. To save the country, Lawless recommended that the legislature at its next session adopt some measures "to punish, if they cannot prevent those exhortations to rebellion and civil war."[6]

Although Lovejoy's newspaper had never been guilty of advocating a slave rebellion, Lawless' widely publicized condemnation served as the signal for overt action against the *Observer.* For the first time in several months a man of prestige, an important civic leader, had spoken publicly against Lovejoy. Thus once again the populace had been given the assurance that men of respectability did not choose to protect Lovejoy's right to disseminate his opinions and would indeed welcome his destruction. On the night of May 23, 1836, someone broke into the newspaper office and stole part of the composing sticks. The next noon, with the printers absent and the office empty, it was entered again and more printing materials stolen. A week later the damage was still greater when an intruder battered the newspaper form.[7] Lovejoy would thus return from Pittsburgh to a city which

. . . . .

[6] *Missouri Republican,* May 26, 1836.

[7] St. Louis *Observer,* June 2, 1836.

contained elements actively hostile toward him and his antislavery views.

At the same time this was happening in St. Louis, a mob in northern Missouri drove Lovejoy's friend, the Reverend David Nelson, out of the state. Since early youth Nelson had opposed slavery, and now he had become an avowed abolitionist. Born in Jonesborough in eastern Tennessee, long a center of antislavery sentiment, he had studied at Washington College under the Reverend Samuel Doak, a teacher who apparently indoctrinated many of his students with an enduring hatred for slavery. After serving as an army surgeon during the War of 1812, he was licensed to preach by the Presbyterian church, and early in 1830 moved to Palmyra, Missouri, where he founded Marion College as a manual labor institution for the training of Presbyterian preachers.[8]

By the mid-1830's, however, the reputation of Marion College was not based on the quality of the preachers it graduated, but rather on its infamy throughout Missouri as a center of abolitionism. It was no secret that Nelson enjoyed a national reputation for his antislavery work, or that Marion College attracted a student body of antislavery zealots. When Nelson attended the Presbyterian general assembly in Pittsburgh in 1835, his antislavery enthusiasm brought him to the attention of Theodore D. Weld, who recommended his appointment as the American Anti-Slavery Society's agent for Missouri.[9] Thus affiliated with the national antislavery movement, he returned to Missouri and promptly entered on the course that was to lead to his expulsion from the state. Already he had acquired the habit of indicting slaveholders with the most vivid language he could command, and he refused to make any effort at all to conciliate those who did not agree with his views. According to his own account, he customarily warned the slaveholders in his congregations that he could not admin-

. . . . .

[8] William A. Richardson, "Dr. David Nelson and His Times," *Journal of the Illinois State Historical Society,* XIII (1920-21), 433-463; Dwight Lowell Dumond, *Antislavery Origins of the Civil War in the United States* (Ann Arbor, Michigan, 1939), pp. 6-7; C. McHovey to the editor, *Home Missionary,* April 13, 1830, AHMS Papers.

[9] American Anti-Slavery Society, Committee on Agencies, Minutes (Boston Public Library); *Dictionary of American Biography,* XIII, 415.

ister the Lord's Supper to them unless they first washed away the blood that dripped from their fingernails.[10]

During the next year the American Anti-Slavery Society elected him one of its vice-presidents, and—so the rumors went—several avowed abolitionists took up residence at the college, where they made antislavery speeches, distributed antislavery publications, and aided slaves to escape to Illinois. Marion College by that time, and with good reason, had gained a reputation as a hotbed of abolitionist activity.[11]

In the spring of 1836 two students arrived bringing with them free Negroes and a library of antislavery materials. This was too much for the people in the neighborhood. A mob soon appeared, captured the Negroes, burned the books, and ordered the offending students to leave. On May 21 the enraged citizens held a public meeting to discuss the abolitionist activity going on around them. The next day at the Greenfield campground five miles from the college, Nelson read from the pulpit an appeal written by William Muldrow, one of the founders of the college, asking for contributions to aid in colonizing free Negroes in Africa. His action led to the meeting breaking up in a riot during which one member of the congregation was stabbed.[12] The entire community was thrown into great confusion as a result, and, according to a local resident, "many hurried to their homes to prepare for war." Public opinion against Nelson raged so furiously that for his own safety he fled to Illinois. There he found refuge in the town of Quincy, where members of the Congregational church sympathetic to antislavery ideas were eager to help him.[13]

This then was the situation when Elijah and Celia Lovejoy returned to St. Louis in the middle of 1836: one mob had dragged a Negro from jail and burned him; another had driven an antislavery clergyman from the state; and the *Observer* had been attacked and damaged. . . . . .

[10] David Nelson to Absalom Peters, September 13, 1837, AHMS Papers.

[11] American Anti-Slavery Society, *Third Annual Report* (New York, 1836), p. 24.

[12] Benjamin G. Merkel, "The Abolition Aspects of Missouri's Antislavery Controversy, 1819-1865," *Missouri Historical Review,* XLIV (1949-50), 244-246; St. Louis *Observer,* June 2, 1836; Alton *Western Pioneer,* August 5, 1836.

[13] George C. Wood to Absalom Peters, June 3, 1836, AHMS Papers; Thomas Pope, "Historical Sketches of the First Half Century of the First Congregational Church of Quincy, Illinois . . . and of the First Union Congregational Church" (unpaged MS., Hammond Library, Chicago Theological Seminary).

Lovejoy knew very well that against so much opposition his efforts would prove totally ineffective. The day when the citizens of a Southern state would tolerate an aggressive antislavery newspaper had apparently passed. Therefore, nothing could be accomplished if he remained in St. Louis. He could best serve the cause of God and man, he decided, by leaving Missouri.

After sending Celia and their son to her mother's home in St. Charles, he began to make plans for moving the *Observer* to Alton. But meanwhile he wanted to express his opinions concerning recent events. He did not have much to say about the expulsion of Nelson. That, after all, was the sort of thing an abolitionist in a slave state must expect. Uppermost in his mind was not Nelson but the proceedings in Judge Lawless' court, which Lovejoy believed involved matters of great principle.

When the judge had made his charge to the grand jury, he had instructed it to return no indictments if it should find that the burning of McIntosh was "not the act of numerable and ascertainable malefactors; but of congregated thousands, seized upon and impelled by that mysterious, metaphysical, and almost electric frenzy, which, in all ages and nations, has hurried on the infuriated multitude to deeds of death and destruction. . . ." If such had been the situation in that lynching, he told the jury, then the matter "transcends your jurisdiction—it is beyond the reach of human law." The jury, apparently deciding that the mob had been seized by an "electric frenzy," returned no indictment, and those who had burned McIntosh went unpunished. Such an interpretation of law seemed to Lovejoy to give carte blanche to mobs, to guarantee them legal immunity.[14]

Lovejoy's printed observation on Judge Lawless' statements did not touch upon the question of slavery. Instead, he once more defended civil rights and condemned mob violence. Even more than that, he again made a strong appeal to Protestant prejudice against foreigners and Catholics. Judge Lawless, Lovejoy observed, was one of Missouri's many "foreigners educated in the old world." Such persons, in Lovejoy's opinion, could never "come to have a proper understanding of Constitutional law." Moreover, he added, "Judge Lawless is a Papist; . . . .

[14] *Missouri Republican,* May 26, 1836.

and in his Charge we see the cloven foot of Jesuitism, peeping out from under the veil of almost every paragraph. . . ."[15]

Lovejoy accompanied these statements with a warning of the implications to be drawn from the doctrine Lawless had promulgated. He had ruled that a mob may be excused from acts that would be punishable under the law if committed by individuals. By this doctrine, warned Lovejoy, "society is resolved into its first elements, and every man must hold his property and his life, at the point of the dagger." It is "subversive of all law," he concluded, and at once opens the door for "the perpetration, by a congregated mob, calling themselves the people, of every species of violence, and that too with perfect impunity."[16]

Lovejoy's editorial proved to be prophetic. Instead of producing sober thought among the citizens, it served only to increase the chances for violence. His remarks offended the Irish, the Catholics, the admirers of Judge Lawless, the members of the mob that had burned McIntosh, and all the other opponents of the *Observer*. The limits of their toleration had at last been exceeded.

As a companion-piece to the editorial against Lawless, Lovejoy had inserted in the columns of the *Observer* a notice of his intention to move the newspaper to Alton, where he would find himself more useful and the paper supported better than in St. Louis. As things turned out, however, it was not possible for him to make any other decision. At midnight on the day the offending article appeared, a crowd of nearly 200 people, antagonized by the continuing boldness of Lovejoy's editorial policy, surrounded the *Observer* office. While the rest watched, about twenty men broke down the door, entered the office, and destroyed $700 worth of printing materials, although they did not injure the press itself.[17]

This event marked the end of Lovejoy's career in St. Louis, for violence of that sort, he knew, could not be controlled once it had started. He had been spared for the present, but it seemed doubtful

. . . . .

[15] St. Louis *Observer*, July 21, 1836.

[16] *Ibid.*

[17] *Missouri Republican*, July 23, 1836; St. Louis *Observer*, August 10, 1836; Alton *Telegraph*, August 27, 1836; Lovejoy to Joseph Lovejoy, July 30, 1836, Lovejoy, *Memoir*, p. 181.

that he could continue unharmed. He must also consider the safety of his wife and son, who might themselves ultimately fall victims to the mob's wrath. With his family secure at St. Charles, Lovejoy spent his last night in St. Louis alone in his silent house. He had prepared to defend himself from attack by strengthening the doors and placing a gun in his bedroom, but in spite of his defenses, he lay in his bed sleepless most of the night, weary and sick from the events of the day and fearful that an assassin might attack him at any moment.[18]

Nonetheless, he entertained no idea of abandoning the antislavery crusade. "I have got the harness on," he declared, "and I do not intend to lay it off, except at His command." But whatever his resolution, he realized the scene of his activities must be changed immediately. Since there was no way of knowing to what extent the violence might reach, he hastened to leave the city. He crated his press at once and put it on a steamboat for later delivery to Alton. He also packed his furniture for shipment, but before that could be loaded, most of it, together with his brother John's belongings, was destroyed by persistent remnants of the mob. He himself fled to safety across the Mississippi River to Alton.[19]

With a feeling of relief Lovejoy set foot on the Illinois shore. Opposition and mob violence had not discouraged him. He was "in fine spirits," reported his brother John: "not the least depressed but rather elevated by recent occurrences."[20] His wife and child were safe in St. Charles. The press would follow on a later boat, and though most of his furniture had been lost, he supposed he could make a new start for himself and his family in that friendly, free state. Several antislavery centers already flourished in Illinois—most conspicuously in Quincy, under the influence of David Nelson, and in Springfield, Peoria, and Jacksonville. From these sources he expected to receive support for his newspaper and for his antislavery opinions.

There was every reason, then, to suppose that the thriving city of Alton would afford a hospitable setting for the publication of the *Observer* and a congenial home for the family of a Presbyterian re-

. . . . .

[18] Lovejoy to Elizabeth Lovejoy, August 31, 1836 (Chicago Historical Society).

[19] *Ibid.;* Lovejoy to Joseph Lovejoy, July 30, 1836, Lovejoy, *Memoir,* p. 182; John Lovejoy to Elizabeth Lovejoy, July 26, 1836, Wickett-Wiswall Collection.

[20] John Lovejoy to Elizabeth Lovejoy, July 26, 1836, Wickett-Wiswall Collection.

former. On several occasions he had talked with representative citizens of the city who had assured him that he and his newspaper would be welcome among them. His brother John, who had worked in the office of the Alton *Telegraph,* had given only good reports of the city; and his close friend and antislavery associate in the presbytery of St. Louis, the Reverend Thaddeus Beman Hurlbut, who had recently moved to Alton, reported that sentiment appeared to favor the establishment of the *Observer* there.[21]

But before Lovejoy had been in Illinois many hours, he was given cause to wonder whether even a free state would provide a place of refuge, whether it would be possible ever to escape the hostility that had plagued him in Missouri. Contrary to his instructions, the steamboat *Palmyra* had delivered his printing press to the wharf at Alton on Sunday morning, July 24. Unwilling to remove it on the Sabbath, he had allowed it to lie there unattended all that day. Early the next morning a messenger knocked at his door to bring alarming news. Sometime three or four hours before dawn, he reported, a handful of men, supposedly from Missouri, had damaged the press and shoved it into the river.[22]

By noon news of this latest outrage had spread throughout Alton, arousing sympathy for Lovejoy and indignation that his property should have been destroyed while it lay within the bounds of a law-abiding city. Although riots were not unheard of in Alton, this was not the sort of thing one expected to have happen there. Two months before, a mob had stormed the rooms of Mr. Schweighoofer, a "magical professor," and demolished his instruments. But the leaders had been fined $100, and the city had soon resumed its usual sober character, which the townspeople liked to think contrasted notably with that of the neighboring city across the river. Upon hearing that Lovejoy's press had been destroyed, a group of Alton's leading citizens, their civic pride injured, called a mass meeting for Monday evening to assure Lovejoy that such events as had occurred that morning did

. . . . .

[21] John Lovejoy to Owen Lovejoy, March 27, 1836, Owen Lovejoy Papers; Minutes of the Presbytery of Illinois, New School, 1832-70, II, 131 (McCormick Theological Seminary, Chicago); St. Louis *Observer,* March 10, 1836.

[22] Alton *Observer,* September 8, 1836.

not have their approval and would not be countenanced in the future.[23]

The people who assembled that night in the newly constructed Presbyterian church were anxious to do what was right. They wanted to prove to Lovejoy and to all others who might hear of the incident that they would maintain the law in Alton. Yet, they were conservative men, not much opposed to slavery; and since all of them knew of Lovejoy's reputation, they did not wish to suggest by protecting him that they were abolitionists. Many of those present at the meeting were suspicious of him and his intentions. After all, there had been much trouble and many frightening accusations made against him while he lived in St. Louis. Consequently, before taking any action, they requested Lovejoy to explain to them his position on slavery and to discuss his plans for conducting his newspaper in their city.

Lovejoy stood up in the church, lighted only by the twilight of the July evening, to present himself to the leading citizens of the town in which he had decided to live. He must state his views with perfect clarity. If possible, he must avoid offending anyone; but while reassuring his audience, he must also be certain not to compromise his integrity. In careful phrases he began. First of all, he explained, he was not an abolitionist in the sense they understood the word; that is, he did not advocate turning the slaves loose upon society without first preparing them for freedom. Yet he was an "uncompromising enemy of Slavery, and so expected to live and so to die." As for the policy of the *Observer* now that he had moved it to Alton, he intended it henceforth to be primarily a religious journal. He expected to give much less room to slavery than he had in the past, though he warned that he reserved the right to publish whatever he might choose on any subject or to change his views at any time.[24]

Despite the undoubted effectiveness of this speech, Lovejoy probably never made a more unfortunate public statement, for it was filled with

. . . . .

[23] Alton *Telegraph,* May 11, August 27, 1836; Edward Beecher, *Narrative,* p. 18.

[24] Lovejoy's own version of his statements at this meeting is in his letter to Joseph Lovejoy, July 30, 1836, Lovejoy, *Memoir,* pp. 181-182. A similar version attested to by ten prominent citizens who attended the meeting is in Lovejoy, *Memoir,* pp. 221-222.

half-truths and ambiguities. Furthermore, it reflected Lovejoy's apparent misunderstanding of his own character. He denied being an abolitionist; yet he was an abolitionist in precisely the same sense that Theodore D. Weld and James G. Birney and a thousand other Western antislavery men were abolitionists. To refuse to call himself by that term was to deny to words their proper meaning and to mislead and confuse his listeners. Neither should he have told his audience that "now having come to a free state where [slavery] does not exist, I feel myself less called upon to discuss the subject than when I was in St. Louis." He surely ought to have recognized that he had progressed so far into the antislavery movement that for a man of his temperament there could be no turning back and no standing still. To be sure, he also candidly confessed his continued abhorrence of slavery, and he specifically reserved for himself the right of complete editorial freedom—"I shall hold myself at liberty to speak, to write, and to publish whatever I please on any subject," he had said. But this reservation must have carried far less import to those who heard it that night than did his forecast that he would henceforth feel "less called upon to discuss" slavery.[25]

No doubt Lovejoy sincerely believed that he would now lessen his emphasis on slavery, but by saying so, he betrayed a serious lack of self-understanding. If the people of Alton should agree with him about the iniquity of slavery, he would certainly have little need to emphasize his abolitionist views in the *Observer;* but suppose, instead, that they should refuse to accept his ideas, refuse to join antislavery societies, refuse publicly to condemn slavery. Would his concept of duty allow him then to remain silent? Was Judge Lawless not correct when he told the St. Louis jury a few months earlier that abolitionists seemed "to consider themselves as special agents . . . in fact, of Divine Providence"? Did he not penetrate to the heart of their mission when he observed that "they seem to have their eyes fixed on some mystic vision—some Zion . . . within whose holy walls they would impound us all, or condemn us to perish on the outside"?

. . . . .

[25] The Rev. John Mason Peck, who was present to hear Lovejoy's speech, wrote a year later that Lovejoy had "solemnly pledged" that the *Observer* "was not to be an abolition press. . . ." Peck to John Stevens, August 29, 1837, Stevens Collection (American Baptist Historical Library, Rochester, New York).

But in spite of those shortcomings which we now see, the men who heard Lovejoy on that occasion were completely satisfied with his explanation—he did not belong in the camp of the extreme abolitionists, and his newspaper would no longer emphasize slavery. In fact, Lovejoy's speech had been so convincing that some who had not fully comprehended the import of his words mistakenly believed afterward that he had given them an ironclad promise to abandon his antislavery campaign. He had, of course, done no such thing; and, in any case, he had specifically reserved the right to speak freely on slavery or any other subject. But, understandably, that was not the impression most of his audience received. When the people of Alton later discovered that he had continued to oppose slavery, their wrath toward him became so much the greater because they believed they had been deceived. Lovejoy, it seemed to them, had abused their hospitality and broken a solemn pledge.

However, all of that lay in the future. Having seen Lovejoy and having heard him speak, they were convinced that he was not a radical but a chastened reformer who could be counted upon to give no further trouble. Accordingly they passed resolutions promising to sustain the laws, to ferret out the offenders who had destroyed the press, and to reimburse Lovejoy for his loss. Then they proceeded to leave no doubt that they disapproved of abolitionist doctrines. They would, they said, exercise their influence "in all lawful ways to prevent the publication" of any abolitionist newspaper in Alton.[26]

If Lovejoy were struck by the ominous sound of the last resolution, he did not show it. As he walked out of the Presbyterian church into the summer night, he appeared satisfied with the events of the evening and warmed by the promise of support given him by the leading citizens of the city that was to be his new home.

. . . . .

[26] Alton *Telegraph,* August 27, 1836; John G. Gill, "Elijah Lovejoy's Pledge of Silence," *Missouri Historical Society Bulletin,* XIV (January, 1958), 167-177, concludes that Lovejoy did not make such a pledge.

Settling in Illinois

Chapter IX

Lovejoy had satisfied the townspeople as to his conservatism with the remarks he made to the meeting in the Presbyterian church. Most of them were contented with the mistaken idea that the principal theme of the *Observer* from then on would be religion. Thus backed by the good will of the leading citizens of Alton, he made plans to resume the publication of his newspaper.

As he did so, he could congratulate himself on his good fortune to be located at last in so enlightened a community. Here for the first time since he left New England, he found himself living among people whom he understood and who both understood and appreciated him. From all appearances he could hardly have discovered any city in the West better suited as a place to carry on his activities, for at Alton seemed to center much of the humanitarian and religious impulse on which the reform movement was nourished. An influential group of New Englanders who shared his own concern with religion and morality dominated the city. Although the part of Alton bordering on the Mississippi River contained a large Southern-born population, which generally remained loyal to Southern institutions, practically all the town's businessmen had come from either New York or New England. Upper Alton, a village lying two and a half miles east of the river, was the home of many of the benevolent societies' agents who for years had worked side by side with Lovejoy in reform causes.

Naturally local support for Lovejoy was not unanimous. Like most Western communities, Alton possessed its share of people who were antagonistic toward the brand of Puritan morality he represented. A large number of laborers had recently flocked to the city seeking work in the flurry of construction encouraged by the boom of 1836 and 1837. Alton, too, supplied many jobs in its slaughter houses (25,000 hogs were processed there in 1836) and in its yards for the building and repairing of steamboats.[1] Such workers tended to be hostile toward Negroes and to fear economic competition from them. On that account they were not likely to listen approvingly to those who talked about freeing the slaves. There were other grounds for resenting Lovejoy. Probably the men who gathered near the river front in the coffeehouses on Second Street sometimes cursed him for trying to impose his New England ways on people who liked a free-and-easy life. Some merchants, too, whose chief interest lay in maintaining the good will of customers in the South did not relish the idea of sheltering an abolitionist refugee within their city, no matter what assurances he might have given about changing his ways. And, of course, there were in Alton as everywhere else men and women who for reasons of their own—family background, racial prejudice, or simply conservative disposition—opposed all antislavery agitation. But in the summer of 1836 such dissenters in Alton kept their peace, for their sentiments were overruled by those of the dominant group, who welcomed Lovejoy's presence.[2]

Everything in Alton seemed to work to his advantage and to the advantage of the antislavery movement. The leaders of the Presbyterian church and the prominent businessmen of the city, looking upon him as a spokesman for their interests, expressed their concern for his welfare in tangible ways. Now that he faced the problem of raising money to replace his wrecked printing press, two of Alton's wealthy merchants, Benjamin Godfrey, an old sea captain, and his partner, Winthrop S. Gilman, came forth to supply the necessary aid, partly from their own funds and partly from a loan arranged with the Alton branch of the state bank in which they were officers.

. . . . .

[1] For descriptions of Alton see *Illinois in 1837: A Sketch Descriptive . . . of the State of Illinois* (Philadelphia, Pennsylvania, 1837), pp. 113, 115, 129; and John Mason Peck, *A New Guide for Emigrants to the West* (Boston, 1836), p. 302.

[2] Thomas Ford, *A History of Illinois from Its Commencement as a State in 1818 to 1847* (Chicago, 1854), p. 229; George Turnbull Moore Davis, *Autobiography of the Late Col. Geo. T. M. Davis* (New York, 1891), p. 50

Godfrey and Gilman played approximately the same role in the Illinois reform movement that the Tappan brothers played in the East. When the directors of some local philanthropic society needed a financial contribution to carry on their work, they usually appealed to Godfrey and Gilman. When a congregation wanted to build a new church, they sooner or later directed their fund-raising efforts toward the well-filled pockets of Godfrey and Gilman, and seldom were they disappointed. The spacious stone Presbyterian church that lifted its white spire above the streets of Alton was the latest and most impressive monument to Godfrey and Gilman's philanthropy.[3]

So with a wallet containing money supplied by these merchant philanthropists. Lovejoy left by steamboat to purchase a new printing press in Cincinnati.[4] His brother John, staying behind to look after Celia and her infant son, made plans to protect the new establishment. "I shall watch it now," he told his mother, "and the first person that attempts to come to harm it, may expect a small piece of lead to be lodged in him, for it is of no use to trifle with these scoundrels."[5]

While Lovejoy gathered printing materials and made plans to set up his new office, he found plenty of time to reflect on past events and to consider future action. If he were ever going to abandon his antislavery views, now was the time to do it. Experience had taught him that defending such sentiments held mortal danger, that their publication could lead to social upheaval and to disaster for himself and his family. Expediency dictated that he forget about the slave and concentrate instead on such less-opposed causes as temperance and the establishment of Sunday schools. By so doing, he could expect to live a quiet, useful life in Alton. His newspaper probably would prosper, his family would be well cared for, respected, and secure. But he rejected all these considerations and wavered not at all from his earlier purpose. The events of the summer had not deflected him from his course. If anything, he had become even more determined in opposing slavery. "The cry of the oppressed has entered not only into my ears, but into my soul," he declared, "so that while I live I cannot hold my peace."[6]

. . . . .

[3] Theron Baldwin to Absalom Peters, June 30, 1836, AHMS Papers.

[4] Lovejoy to Elizabeth Lovejoy, August 31, 1836 (Chicago Historical Society).

[5] John Lovejoy to Elizabeth Lovejoy, September 4, 1836, Wickett-Wiswall Collection.

[6] Lovejoy to Elizabeth Lovejoy, August 31, 1836 (Chicago Historical Society).

By this time, Lovejoy looked upon himself as being a figure of importance in the national antislavery movement and upon the continuation of the *Observer* as being vital to the success of the antislavery cause in America. But personal considerations of a different sort also required him to remain resolute. When the preachers and the reformers gave Lovejoy their approval and their money, they received from him in return a commitment, tacit perhaps, but nonetheless firm. In accepting their support, he assured them he would continue the struggle to re-establish his newspaper and to agitate in the antislavery interest. Should he abandon the position he had taken, he would thereby betray the trust of men whose approval he sought and valued. Failure to persist in his antislavery stand would certainly involve abandoning those religious ideals which had thus far given his life meaning. It would probably also lead to his rejection by the social and intellectual groups to which he belonged. To retreat from his position would be to risk the ignominy suffered by the "dark deniers," those early Christians who denied their faith under the torments of persecution. Burdened with such knowledge, Lovejoy could persevere in his course more easily and with less spiritual anguish than he could abandon it.

Few people in Alton yet realized the degree of Lovejoy's devotion to the antislavery cause. Some, bemused by their misinterpretation of his remarks at the public meeting held the day after he arrived in Alton, supposed he intended to abandon his antislavery efforts altogether. They could not have been more mistaken. And Lovejoy at once set about correcting the error. In an extra issue of the *Observer* published two weeks after his appearance before the assembled citizens he repeated some of the remarks he had made on that occasion: "as I stated to the meeting, as I have before stated many times, and as I here repeat, I am opposed to slavery; believing it to be a great moral, and of course, political evil, a sin and a curse to any community where it exists. I believe it to be the duty of every man, on all proper occasions to raise his voice against it, and by all proper and lawful means to endeavor to effect its peaceful removal from among us. Farther than this I have never said, and less than this I never mean to say."

In the first regular issue of the *Observer* published at Alton, he attempted to make his position still clearer. "The system of American negro Slavery is an awful evil and sin . . . ," he wrote, "and it is the duty of us all . . . to effect the speedy and entire emancipation of that portion of our fellow-men in bondage amongst us. . . . " Never, he announced, would he yield to mob pressure against "the rights of conscience, the freedom of opinion, and of the press." For support in maintaining his right to publish his views, he appealed to the "friends of Truth, of Order, of the Rights of Conscience, and of God." Thus, on the day the new *Observer* first appeared in Alton, its readers ought to have understood that Lovejoy had not retreated in his antislavery course. He still believed slavery a sin, he still thought all men obligated to work for its extinction, and he still maintained his perfect right to print those beliefs freely, no matter how distasteful some of the public might find them.[7]

Not everyone, of course, supposed or hoped that Lovejoy had altered his position. The officials of the Presbyterian and Congregational churches assumed that the *Observer,* transplanted to a free state, would continue to advocate the abolition of slavery, and on that basis they had welcomed Lovejoy to Illinois. When the Presbyterian synod of Illinois met at Alton in October, 1836, it went on record in support of his program. Already permeated with antislavery sentiment, the synod resolved that "efforts ought to be immediately made to convince the members of our church, that, to hold our fellows . . . as property, is a heinous sin, against God." Nor did the synod limit itself to an expression of merely theoretical support. Just before it adjourned, fourteen members announced their willingness to pay any debts the *Observer* might incur during its next two years of publication.[8] The Congregational association went even further in sentiment than the Presbyterians. It proclaimed slavery a "heinous sin" calling for immediate repentance, demanded reparation to the slaves "for the wrongs heaped upon them," expressed sympathy for the antislavery leaders who had "so undeservedly experienced" persecution, and recommended the *Observer* to the patronage of the Congregationalists in Illinois.[9]

. . . . .

[7] Alton *Observer,* August 10 (extra), September 8, 1836.

[8] Minutes of the Synod of Illinois, New School, 1831-69, I, 84-85 (McCormick Theological Seminary, Chicago); Alton *Observer,* November 24, 1836, January 26, 1837.

[9] "Minutes of the Congregational Association of Illinois, 1835-1840," William W. Sweet (ed.), *The Congregationalists, 1783-1850* (Chicago, 1939), pp. 177-178.

Probably most people in Alton itself, no matter what their views on slavery, sympathized in theory with Lovejoy's right to publish his newspaper; yet only a minority of them subscribed to it or contributed money for its support. The pledge they had made at the July meeting to reimburse Lovejoy for the loss of his first press was never kept. The first issue of the Alton *Observer* went to fewer than 1,000 subscribers, and Lovejoy's financial outlook appeared so bleak that his family back in Maine proposed to send him money to help keep the paper going. The long-range prospect was not so gloomy, however. Lovejoy's agents numbered twenty-four, distributed throughout nineteen counties in northern Illinois. He was employing John Viall to travel around the state gathering subscriptions. Backed by this kind of organization and supported by two large religious denominations, the newspaper would surely flourish, provided only that Illinois contained a population sympathetic to a militant reform newspaper.[10]

Fortunately for Lovejoy such sympathizers already lived in the state. The northern and central parts of Illinois were rapidly being settled by emigrants from the Northeast, many of whom shared his religious interest and moral point of view. "Most of the Xians of our Church are from New England," wrote Jeremiah Porter from Chicago in 1833, "& of course are awake to the benevolent plans of the day." Some of these new settlers had moved from their homes in the East filled with a sense of exalted mission similar to Lovejoy's. "Why came we to the West," asked one of them. "Were we not in a measure set apart *to do good?*" The names of such men and women were easily added to the subscription list of Lovejoy's newspaper, their aid thus enlisted in the antislavery cause.[11]

This was the kind of public for whom Lovejoy edited the *Observer,* and at his office in Alton he computed the statistics that proved the public responded. The newspaper's circulation steadily increased. He announced that during the last week in October, 1836, his agents had sent him eighty new subscriptions. By the middle of March, 1837, cir-

. . . . .

[10] Lovejoy, *Memoir,* p. 187; Elizabeth Lovejoy to Owen Lovejoy, September 29, 1836, Owen Lovejoy Papers; Alton *Observer,* September 8 and 29, 1836.

[11] "Evangelism in Chicago—1833, a Letter Written by Jeremiah Porter," *Bulletin of the Chicago Historical Society,* II (1936-39), 35; Frances Willard to Julius Willard, January 29, 1840, Samuel Willard Papers (Illinois State Historical Library, Springfield).

culation had risen to more than 1,700. Before publication ceased a few months later, it had exceeded 2,000.[12]

With his newspaper already established more solidly in Illinois than it had ever been in Missouri, Lovejoy entered wholeheartedly into the civil life of Alton. Here, unlike St. Louis, the community accepted him and appreciated his work. Alton had no lyceum for the discussion of public issues, so Lovejoy organized one, recruited some fifty members, and served as its first president. Not only did he serve as the focus of the existing reform movement, but his presence also stimulated additional reform activity in the city. In the fall of 1836, the local newspaper announced, as though symbolizing the arrival in Alton of the leading representative of the benevolent movement in the area, that all the annual meetings of the reform societies previously held at the state capital would henceforth convene in the Presbyterian church at Alton. Beginning on November 29 and meeting on successive days, conventions were held there by the Illinois Bible Society, the Illinois Sunday School Union, the Illinois Temperance Society, and the Illinois Tract Society.[13]

Such a circumstance could serve only to benefit Lovejoy. Dozens of prominent ministers and laymen from all over the state flocked to Alton late in November to attend these conventions. Inevitably most of the delegates who had not yet met Lovejoy were eager to become acquainted with such a well-known champion of freedom for the slave and freedom of the press. Despite Lovejoy's prominence, however, to the ministers who came to Alton he appeared not so much an object of curiosity as simply a fellow worker in a common enterprise. On that basis, they were eager to talk with him about his experiences in Missouri and about his problems and plans for the future. Such contacts encouraged Lovejoy to continue in the course he had set for himself. Clerical approval created pressure upon him, but this was reciprocal. Should the need ever develop, he could confidently suppose that these men would be counted among his defenders and adherents in the cause of abolition and free speech.

. . . . .

[12] Alton *Observer,* October 27, 1836, February 16, March 16, 1837; Lovejoy, *Memoir,* p. 187; Lovejoy to Joseph Lovejoy, April 14, 1837, Wickett-Wiswell Collection.
[13] Alton *Telegraph,* November 9 and 23, 1836.

In spite of all the unaccustomed support Lovejoy received, the growing prosperity of the antislavery movement in Illinois did not go unchallenged. The Baptists of southern Illinois attempted to revive interest in the colonization of Negroes in Africa as a means of opposing the idea of immediate emancipation. "In proportion as the schemes of the Abolitionists are seen to be visionary," wrote James Lemen, the spearhead of the Illinois colonization movement, "this much abused enterprise is rising again in public favor. . . . " So it was, and this time it rose in conscious opposition to the newly formed antislavery societies. Lovejoy and most other abolitionists saw no objection to sending freed slaves to Africa if they wanted to go there. Rather, they scored the American Colonization Society for its ineffectiveness in solving the basic problem involved in American slavery. Abolitionists regarded the operation of the colonization societies as a means of evading a fundamental moral issue.[14]

The colonizationists were not the only group in Illinois trying to channel support away from the abolitionists. In some circles men already were talking about passing laws to prevent the abolitionists from spreading their ideas at all. Early in December, 1836, before Lovejoy had been in Illinois six months, the Alton Literary Society debated the question, "Is it the duty of the people of Illinois, by legislative enactment to prohibit the circulation of abolitionist doctrine in the state?"[15]

Rumblings were soon heard also in the state capital, where both houses of the General Assembly took up the issue of abolition. From the reformers' point of view, the state legislators were a sorry lot anyway, and their action in this matter seemed only to confirm their corruption. Lovejoy's patron, old Benjamin Godfrey of Alton, happened to be in the capital at that time. What he saw appalled him. "This is now a terrible place," he wrote, with "Greate Room for Reform." The voters had failed to give enough attention to the moral characters of the men they elected, he decided.[16]

On New Year's Day, 1837, Senator Orville H. Browning presented

. . . . .

[14] Alton *Western Pioneer,* July 22, 1836; Alton *Observer,* February 27, 1837.

[15] Alton *Telegraph,* December 7, 1836.

[16] Benjamin Godfrey to Theron Baldwin, January 5, 1837 (Illinois State Historical Library).

a committee report to the General Assembly branding the purposes of the abolitionists as "highly reprehensive" and dangerous to the Union. Abolitionist activities, the committee said, had not helped the slave; they had only made his lot harder than it had been. Even worse, the abolitionists stirred up discord between the sections and violence in the communities where they operated. Although Browning's committee did not recommend legislative action against the abolitionists, it expressed the hope that public opinion "would firmly and powerfully pronounce the rebuke which is so richly merited. . . ." If Lovejoy read the committee's report, he may well have asked himself whether the senators had in mind the same kind of rebuke the citizens of St. Louis had pronounced on him a few months earlier when they drove him from the city.[17]

In the Illinois House of Representatives seventy-seven members voted to approve resolutions against antislavery societies. Six legislators, however, refused to accept the resolutions. Among them was Abraham Lincoln. On March 3, 1837, he and Dan Stone, representatives from Sangamon County, entered their protest to the action of the General Assembly. The two concurred in the opinion "that the promulgation of abolition doctrines tends rather to increase than abate" the evils of slavery. But they took the opportunity also to express their view that slavery possessed a moral aspect. Slavery, they maintained, was a system founded on both "injustice and bad policy." The abolitionists had long been saying much the same thing. Obviously, antislavery views were spreading in Illinois no matter how much the state legislators might deplore the fact.[18]

In Alton, as one would expect, people discussed the slavery issue with special interest. Early in January, 1837, the Upper Alton Lyceum—the organization Lovejoy had founded three months earlier—decided to debate the question, "Does the principle of right require the immediate emancipation of the slave?" Lovejoy and the few other abolitionists in Alton had, of course, already made up their minds on that subject, but some people in Alton were quite as convinced that the proper answer to the question was "No." Both groups thus looked

. . . . .

[17] *Illinois Senate Journal,* 10 Gen. Assembly, 1 Sess., pp. 195-198, 297

[18] *Illinois House Journal,* 10 Gen. Assembly, 1 Sess., pp. 241-244, 311, 817-818; Albert J. Beveridge, *Abraham Lincoln, 1809-1858* (Boston, 1928), I, 192-195.

forward to the discussions as a chance to air their particular views and prejudices. Only the uncommitted might expect to be enlightened.

An excited crowd filled the lyceum's meeting hall on the evening of January 19. The members arrived with minds and emotions already charged by the currents of discord this most divisive of public issues generated. Before the discussion had even begun, J. W. Collett, who had succeeded Lovejoy as lyceum president, announced his resignation, explaining to the members that he felt "some delicacy in presiding over the deliberations of the question." Collett took his seat with the rest of the audience, a new president was elected, and the debates began. An outside observer would have concluded that the affirmative had the better of the debate, for with Lovejoy present, who knew the arguments against slavery as well as he knew the Westminster Confession, the opponents of immediate emancipation were outclassed. Nonetheless, the members could reach no decision at the first meeting, and the discussion was continued to the next week.

For two sessions the members discussed the subject, sometimes noisily and almost always with tempers strained. The chairman had all he could do to maintain order during these long meetings that were marked, the secretary noted, by "an unusual display of Parliamentary talent." The discussions practically wrecked the organization. So much controversy was aroused, so many hard feelings provoked, that the membership promptly declined from fifty to twenty-five. At the third meeting, Junius Hall moved to end the discussion. Lovejoy immediately insisted that the topic ought not to be dropped, that not all aspects of the subject had yet been canvassed. But he was overruled. After what the secretary termed an "animated discussion," the members resolved to let the president decide the issue. Debate should cease, he ruled, and despite heated protests, the membership sustained his decision. Lovejoy attended the lyceum's next meeting, but with the imposition of this local gag rule, he did not do so again. His name ceased to appear on the list of members, and for two years the society debated no further aspect of the slavery question.[19]

Although this defeat was in itself a minor thing, it was Lovejoy's first setback in Alton, the first clear evidence he had seen of local opposition. He reacted in predictable fashion. Thus far, since mov-

. . . . .

[19] Journal of the Upper Alton Lyceum (Illinois State Historical Library).

ing to Alton, he had printed antislavery articles only occasionally. But with the development of opposition his views rapidly became more extreme and his expression of them less guarded. Aware that Godfrey and Gilman had given him money to buy his press on the supposition that the *Observer* would be primarily a religious newspaper, he consulted with Gilman about his changed policy. Would the partners countenance the use of the press for the dissemination of extreme antislavery doctrine, he asked. With Gilman indicating no objection, Lovejoy proceeded as his conscience directed, filling his columns with sharp antislavery essays.[20]

A few weeks after the lyceum debates he engaged in a long controversy in the *Observer* over the merits of slavery with the Reverend Asa Cummings, editor of the Portland, Maine, *Christian Mirror*. One of his most vivid condemnations of the institution appeared at that time. What is it to be a slave, he asked. His answer both summarizes important abolitionist argument and illustrates the emotional style that Lovejoy affected: "It is to toil all day . . . with the bitter certainty always before me, that not one cent of what I earn, is, or can be my own. It is to depart from my hut every morning, with the sickening fear, that before I return at night, it will be visited by the slave-driving fiend. . . . My first-born son, denied even the poor privilege of bidding his father farewell, is on his way, a chained and manacled victim, to a distant market, there to be disposed of in shambles, where human flesh and sinews are bought and sold. It is to enter my cabin, and see my wife or daughter struggling in the lustful embraces of my master, or some of his white friends, without daring to attempt their rescue. . . . But above all, to be a slave, is to be denied the privilege of reading the gospel of the Son of God, to have no control over my own children, and, consequently to be deprived of the power and means of educating them in the principles of morality and religion. In one word, it is to be degraded from a man to a brute—to become, instead of a free moral agent, a THING, a piece of property, and to be used as such—to be deprived of all personal and all civil rights—to be shut out from all enjoyment in this world, and all hope in the next."[21]

. . . . .

[20] Beecher, *Narrative,* p. 19.
[21] Lovejoy, *Memoir,* pp. 198-199.

A few issues later, Lovejoy rejected all plans for gradually freeing the slaves or for improving their condition while they remained in slavery. The only right remedy for sin, he insisted, was its immediate, total abandonment.[22]

Lovejoy's strong indictment of slavery and his demand for its abolition slowly turned the weight of public opinion against him. Probably the man in Petersburg, Illinois, who subscribed to the *Observer* unaware that it was an antislavery journal expressed an opinion shared by many. "I never will pay for it," he wrote upon discovering his error, "and the only wish I have upon the subject is, that you, your press and agent, were all in hell."[23]

No longer was sentiment in Alton so preponderantly in his favor as it had been during the winter. By the spring of 1837 one could hear, if he chose to listen, the grossest sort of rumors about Lovejoy's habits and beliefs. He advocated hanging "without judge or jury" all opponents of abolition. He advocated the amalgamation of the races and was even a practicing amalgamationist, the prurient said. He had declared from the pulpit of the Presbyterian church where he preached during the summer of 1837—it was so believed by many who never attended his sermons—that if his wife were to die that day he would marry a Negro before the next Saturday night. While stories of that sort scarcely merited denial, they suggested the nature of the prejudice developing against him.[24]

An increasing number of people in Alton found Lovejoy and the *Observer* annoying. He criticized their easy morality, their drinking, their oaths, their disregard for the Sabbath, and, most irritating of all, he condemned their materialism. When Lovejoy moved to Illinois in the summer of 1836, Alton prospered as one of the fastest growing cities on the Mississippi River, considering itself, with only moderate exaggeration, a trade rival of St. Louis. The movement was already underway which would lead to its incorporation as a city by the Illinois General Assembly on July 31, 1837. Alton had taken its place in the

. . . . .

[22] Alton *Observer,* March 16, 1837.

[23] Spencer Merrill to Lovejoy, April 22, 1837, *ibid.,* May 4, 1837.

[24] J. Russell to Lovejoy, April 29, 1837, Lovejoy Collection; Lovejoy, *Memoir,* p. 212.

booming American economy of the 1830's, and its speculators could see no limits to the spiraling values of its goods and its land.[25]

But then the bubble of speculation burst, and Alton plunged with the rest of the country into the long, gloomy depression that followed the Panic of 1837. With an air of self-righteousness that seemed intolerable to those who suffered from hard times, Lovejoy commented editorially on the panic. He felt no sympathy at all for the suffering of the jobbers, the bankers, the land speculators—representatives of a generation whose values he thought were askew. "Wealth," he wrote, "has been the god after which this nation . . . has gone a whoring." The depression was God's judgment against a people who had ignored His laws. They tolerated slavery, they failed to observe the Sabbath, they reveled in licentiousness and immorality of every kind. Alton's present difficulties were simply "the chastisement of a kind Father," he said, the just reward of a sinful people.[26]

The indictment contained just enough truth to prove irritating to a people who had little comprehension of the economic forces that had contributed to their downfall. Lovejoy's telling them these things only decreased his popularity in Alton. Everyone knew something had gone wrong in the city. Men who had no understanding of the causes of the panic began to suspect that Lovejoy himself was the source of their troubles.

While Lovejoy was losing the good will of an increasing number of Alton citizens, he identified himself still more closely with the American Anti-Slavery Society. In June, 1837, the leadership of the society decided to organize a huge campaign to deluge the United States Congress and the state legislatures with petitions against slavery. As soon as Lovejoy received news of the plan, he published an appeal for volunteers who would circulate such petitions in Illinois. Even the most casual reader could see that his relationship with organized abolition had become intimate indeed.[27]

. . . . .

[25] William T. Norton, *Centennial History of Madison County, Illinois, and Its People, 1812-1912* (Chicago, 1912), I, 471; *Illinois in 1837*, p. 115.

[26] Alton *Observer*, May 25, 1837.

[27] Gilbert Hobbs Barnes and Dwight Lowell Dumond (eds.), *The Letters of Theodore Dwight Weld, Angelina Grimké Weld, and Sarah Grimké, 1822-1844* (New York, 1934), I, 403-405; Alton *Observer*, June 29, 1837.

A week later he took the step that led to the final alienation of the majority of Alton citizens. Had the time not come, he asked in the columns of the *Observer,* to call a convention to form a state antislavery society? The reaction was immediate. Men in Alton had been willing at least to tolerate an antislavery newspaper whose influence was vague and uncertain, but they could not abide the thought of an avowed antislavery organization forming within their city.[28]

Newspapermen from the other side of the river, who still remembered the days when Lovejoy had agitated among them, encouraged his opponents in Alton. The *Missouri Republican* warned the Alton merchants that if Lovejoy were allowed to carry out his plans their trade with Missouri and other slave states would fall off, and migration to Illinois would cease. Southerners, the newspaper declared, would refuse to have business dealings with people who tolerated abolitionists. To merchants in the bleak months of 1837, who looked into empty tills every evening and who watched the decline of the businesses they had labored to build, this argument made sense. Clearly, Lovejoy's activities contributed to hard times. The *Missouri Republican* more than hinted that a happy solution to the problem would be to silence the *Observer* and drive Lovejoy out of the city.[29]

They were mistaken, however, in supposing Lovejoy solely responsible for issuing the call to organize a state antislavery society. He did not do so on his own initiative. For months other abolitionists had been writing to him, urging the use of the *Observer*'s columns for that purpose. James M. Buchanan, a prominent Kentucky abolitionist who had recently moved to nearby Carlinville, had corresponded with Lovejoy on the subject, and David Nelson and other antislavery men in Quincy had urged him to act. The officers of the American Anti-Slavery Society from their headquarters in New York had also applied pressure on the Illinois abolitionists to organize. Lovejoy, seldom given to precipitate acts, had delayed much longer than others thought wise.[30]

. . . . .

[28] Alton *Observer,* July 6, 1837.

[29] *Missouri Republican,* August 28, 1837.

[30] Beecher, *Narrative,* p. 20; James Buchanan to Birney, August 18, 1837, Elizur Wright, Jr., to Birney, August 14, 1837, in Dwight Lowell Dumond (ed.), *The Letters of James Gillespie Birney, 1831-1857* (New York, 1938), I, 414, 416.

But even if Lovejoy did not originate the plan to hold a state antislavery convention, it was he who suffered the consequences. Two days after he printed the proposal, early risers saw handbills, anonymously issued, tacked along the streets of Alton. All citizens, the bills announced, were invited to meet in the Market House to protest the continued publication of the *Observer* in Alton.[31]

On July 11 while Lovejoy proceeded with plans to hold the state antislavery convention, his opponents convened at the Market House. It was an orderly assembly including some of the most important figures in the city. Benjamin Godfrey and Winthrop S. Gilman were not present, nor were the clergymen of Alton there. But several prominent physicians attended, one of them, Dr. J. A. Halderman, serving as chairman. The men who composed the Market House meeting, though angry and belligerent, wore broadcloth and spoke respectably. It was not an assembly of the rabble.

They got down to work quickly. Their main accomplishment was to pass resolutions censuring Lovejoy for advocating doctrines "contrary to the disposition and will of the citizens of Alton." Besides that, they said, he had violated a pledge to cease antislavery activity. They then appointed a special committee to meet with Lovejoy and find out from his own lips whether he intended to persist in printing articles against slavery and to proceed with his plans to form a state antislavery society. Further public action, they announced, would await Lovejoy's reply.[32]

The committee took a long time to accomplish its function, perhaps because its members could not agree among themselves as to exactly what they should demand from Lovejoy. Furthermore Dr. B. K. Hart and Benjamin Godfrey, neither of whom had attended the meeting, had been named to the committee. Hart finally agreed to serve, but Godfrey, still loyal to Lovejoy, refused to have anything to do with the affair. When, after waiting thirteen days, the committee finally performed its appointed task, the members did not confront Lovejoy personally. Instead, they sent him a letter requesting an answer "such as will be satisfactory to the community." The letter, however, was exceedingly respectful, containing no belligerence whatsoever. The

. . . . .

[31] Lovejoy, *Memoir,* p. 216.

[32] Alton *Telegraph,* July 19, 1837.

men who drafted it had purged themselves of every trace of the hostility that had characterized the public meeting. They were men of intelligence and sensibility. Better than most, they recognized the issues involved in the difficult situation that had developed at Alton.[33]

Their dilemma was the dilemma of the majority in Alton—basically decent men who adhered neither to proslavery nor to abolitionist groups, who were, in fact, apparently incapable of moral commitment. What course ought they to follow when confronted with the advocate of doctrines which envisioned radical social change? They knew that Lovejoy possessed the right granted him by the Constitution to advocate the abolition of slavery. They knew too that he based his antislavery arguments on the religious teachings of the Bible and the natural-rights doctrine of the Declaration of Independence. As nineteenth-century Americans they could not dismiss either of these works or take them lightly. Yet, if they accepted Lovejoy's views and if they allowed antislavery agitation to continue, social upheaval and sectional strife, they believed, might result. On the other hand, if they rejected his views and silenced him, they would thereby deny their religious and political heritage.

The letter they addressed to Lovejoy reflected their intellectual problem. At no point did it even hint that Lovejoy had erred in his arguments or that he did not possess the right to pursue his editorial work in Alton. Indeed, the letter was apologetic in tone. Expressing the "utmost deference" to Lovejoy's "feelings as a man" and to his "rights as a citizen," the committee requested a reply to the resolutions passed at the Market House meeting of July 11. "Nothing," they added, "but the importance of the question which the meeting was called to consider, and the dangers which its unwise agitation threatens, not only to the community, but to the whole country, could have induced us to take the step we have."[34]

When Lovejoy opened the letter and read it for the first time, he already knew his answer. If the people who had attended the meeting imagined that their combined influence could sway Lovejoy, they misjudged him. Any of his friends or associates could have told the men who drafted the letter that they wasted their time. It was far too

. . . . .

[33] Lovejoy, *Memoir,* pp. 225-227.

[34] *Ibid.,* p. 226.

late in Lovejoy's career to expect him to yield to popular pressure, however strong. St. Louis had been his testing ground; there he had faced the crisis and passed it. If popular opposition could crush him, it would have crushed him then. The scenes at the Market House were, after all, merely another rehearsal of a drama he had already played, and he did not intend at that late date to change his part.

The issue was now one of civil rights precisely as it had been the year before in St. Louis, and Lovejoy's response was the same as it had been then. He would gladly open his newspaper columns to anyone who wished to criticize his position, he said, so that both sides might contest for the public mind, but he could not recognize the right of a public meeting to determine his editorial policy. To do so, he added, would be to abrogate the sacred freedom of expression, which did not originate with our forefathers, but "comes to us . . . from our Maker, and is in its nature inalienable, belonging to man as man."[35]

The issue was clear and the lines were drawn. There could be no doubt about Lovejoy's determination to hold fast to his course. If the people of Alton as steadfastly opposed him, the result, however long delayed, would be a dreadful one.

. . . . .

[35] Lovejoy to B. K. Hart and others, July 26, 1837, *ibid.*, pp. 227-229.

Increasing Hostility

Chapter X

Lovejoy made no move whatsoever to placate his opponents in Alton. He did not even condescend to deny their charge that he had pledged to cease his antislavery publication, although ten prominent citizens were willing to affirm that he had not done so. It appeared to him as well as to other abolitionists that great religious, moral, and political principles—the very principles upon which the Republic was based—were at stake in their struggle to discuss slavery. To compromise or to yield their claims to freedom of speech and freedom of the press, they believed, would be a dereliction of personal duty, and to do so would weaken all freedom in America. Therefore neither Lovejoy nor James Buchanan nor any other Illinois abolitionist was willing to alter his program in the interest of tranquillity. The majority in Alton would have to accommodate themselves to Lovejoy; he refused even to recognize them. He calmly proceeded with plans to hold the state antislavery convention as though the Market House meeting had never been held. At the same time he continued to discuss slavery and abolition freely in the columns of the *Observer*.[1]

An event hardly calculated to soothe the public mind was the organization of the Madison County Anti-Slavery Society at Alton early in August, less than a month after the Market House meeting had condemned all such groups. Since Lovejoy served as chairman of the organizational meetings, those who read the newspaper accounts of the

. . . . .

[1] Alton *Observer,* July 20, 1837; Lovejoy, *Memoir,* pp. 221-222.

proceedings inevitably—and correctly—assumed that Lovejoy was largely responsible for its existence.[2]

The members of the new society made no effort to keep their activities or their aims secret, no effort to lessen the impact their organization was certain to have on the already-inflamed public mind in Alton. Indeed, they appeared openly defiant of the opposition that attended their action. In the face of declared hostility, they endorsed the plan to form a state antislavery society and, with obvious reference to Lovejoy and the *Observer,* made a special point of insisting that abolitionists possessed the right conferred by God and guaranteed by the Constitution to attempt to influence public opinion by freely expressing their ideas about slavery or any other subject.[3]

The proceedings of the Madison County Anti-Slavery Society illustrated the direction the antislavery movement throughout the entire country had lately taken. Under the pressure of increased opposition, the abolitionists had shifted their goals. No longer was the antislavery movement solely an effort to restore rights to the slave. It had become an effort also to preserve the civil rights of white men, whose rights to petition, to assemble, to use the mails, to speak, and to publish were daily assaulted by those who feared the results of an open examination of the institution of slavery.

Nowhere in the North in 1837 were those rights more in jeopardy, more perilously maintained, than in Alton. Not only was Lovejoy required to defend himself against local opponents; he had also to face continued antagonism from across the river in Missouri. For weeks in the summer of 1837, the *Missouri Republican* attempted to stir up wrath against him. Late in July it commented that by his antislavery articles he had "merited the full measure of the community's indignation" and "forfeited all claims to the protection of that or any other community." In August it advised the people of Alton that "every consideration for their own and their *neighbor's* prosperity [required them] to stop the course of the *Observer*."[4]

Such remarks were plainly designed to be powerful appeals for mob action; there was nothing subtle about them. Probably the only reason

. . . . .

[2] Alton *Observer,* August 17, 1837.

[3] *Ibid.*

[4] *Missouri Republican,* July 17, August 25, 1837.

violence against Lovejoy had not occurred in Illinois was that the leaders of public opinion had not yet openly withdrawn their protection from him and his newspaper. So long as they upheld law and order, the unruly element would take no action; but let respectable men once suggest that they too wished the *Observer* silenced, then others would come forth to perform the deed. Soon the invitation was given.

Alton had been incorporated as a city only a few days before Lovejoy organized the Madison County Anti-Slavery Society. During the next month while a political campaign was underway for the election of the first city officials, the voters began to investigate the candidates' views on public issues. Shortly after the middle of August at a Whig political meeting in Union Hall, party members directed questions toward Charles Howard, Whig candidate for mayor. Weren't the abolitionists correct, someone asked, in their claim to a constitutional right to publish their opinions? Howard had prepared himself for that question. Putting down abolitionist sentiment, he replied, destroyed not the freedom of the press but rather its licentiousness. At about the same time, Dr. B. K. Hart, whom the Democrats were thinking of nominating for mayor, publicly expressed his doubts about Lovejoy's right to publish his newspaper contrary to the wishes of the majority in Alton. Prominent politicians, spokesmen for the local Whig and Democratic parties, had thus indicated that they probably would not oppose efforts to destroy the *Observer*. Support for Lovejoy had been seriously undermined—the mob was now free to act.[5]

Twice small hostile crowds gathered around Lovejoy's office. The first time, so many journeymen printers and others were inside that the would-be assailants left without attempting any violence. At the second attempt, a heavy rainstorm drove the crowd away. But on Monday night, August 21, between ten and eleven o'clock, a band of perhaps fifteen determined men gathered outside the office and began throwing stones through the windows and shouting threats and insults at the workers inside.[6]

. . . . .

[5] Norton, *Centennial History,* I, 471; Alton *Telegraph,* September 27, 1837.

[6] Lovejoy, *Memoir,* p. 231; Boston *Liberator,* September 15, 1837; New York *Plaindealer,* quoted in Philadelphia *Genius of Universal Emancipation,* XV (1837), 87. The *Genius* was an antislavery periodical edited by Benjamin Lundy.

No law enforcement officials appeared to halt the disturbance. The large group of citizens—"gentlemen of property and standing"—who gathered to watch the proceedings made no effort to restore order. Only one person attempted even a gesture in that direction. He addressed the mob, urging them to give up their plans. Wait until morning, he suggested, when tempers had cooled; then they could "peacefully" pack up the printing materials and put them and the editor on a boat headed toward the South. But not even that counsel of moderation, if it could be called such, was heeded. When it became clear to those inside the office that the people milling around outside were not simply demonstrating but intended to break into the building, they gave up all thought of defending the press and fled to safety. The mob then entered the deserted office and destroyed the press, the type, and other printing materials.[7]

Lovejoy was not in the newspaper office when the mob gathered. Mrs. Lovejoy was ill, as she often had been that summer, and he had stayed at home with her all day. In the evening he had left the house, however, to perform a marriage ceremony a short distance outside of town. On the way home after he had stopped at a drugstore to purchase medicine for his wife, he met the mob on the Huntersville Road at the outskirts of the city. Before they recognized him, he was in their midst. When they realized whom they had surrounded, they threatened to tar and feather the "damned abolitionist." Completely at their mercy, Lovejoy asked only that before they did anything to him they first take the medicine to his wife. This they promised to do, and sent one of their members away with it. Lovejoy then turned to those who threatened him.

"You had better let me go home," he warned. "You have no right to detain me; I have never injured you." But, in the same spirit of resignation that had guided him through all earlier crises, he added, "I am in your hands, and you must do with me whatever God permits you to do."

As Lovejoy became more deeply involved with the organized antislavery movement, he adopted Garrison's principle of nonresistance. He was encouraged in this by his mother, who advised him to clothe himself in the armor of the Lord.[8] Few Western abolitionists followed

. . . . .

[7] Lovejoy, *Memoir*, p. 231.

[8] Elizabeth Lovejoy to Lovejoy [1837], Wickett-Wiswall Collection.

Garrison on this point, and Lovejoy was soon to abandon the principle. For the moment, however, it served him well. That kind of passive resistance—no effort to run, no attempt at physical defense, only an oblique reference to the consciences of his assailants—proved too much for them. After brief consultation, they released him unharmed. They went on, however, to destroy the printing press.[9]

The men who destroyed Lovejoy's press apparently bore no personal hatred for him, nor did some of them even read his newspaper. Yet he was, they knew, an abolitionist whose doctrines they had been taught to fear and to hate even if they did not comprehend them. While the merchants of Alton feared Lovejoy's disruptive influence on their trade relations, the more general hatred for Lovejoy and the *Observer* resulted from widespread fear of the Negro and misunderstanding of abolitionist doctrine. Many ordinary men in that day supposed that the Negro was an inferior order of creation who must be held in subjection for the safety of white society. Abolitionists, they believed, disregarded that "fact" and deliberately encouraged slaves to throw off their yokes and rise against their masters. Both misconceptions were deliberately inculcated in the public mind by men who ought to have known better. Only a few months after the mob had destroyed the *Observer* for the second time, the Attorney General of Illinois, Usher F. Linder, referred publicly to Lovejoy's press "brought here to teach rebellion and insurrection to the slave; to excite servile war; to preach murder in the name of religion; to strike dismay to the hearts of the people, and spread desolation over the face of this land."[10]

The results of the continued circulation of the *Observer* as Linder portrayed them would be dreadful indeed. "I might depict to you the African," he warned, "his passions excited by the doctrines intended to have been propagated by that press. As well might you find yourself in the fangs of a wild beast. I might portray to you the scenes which would exist in our neighbor states from the influence of that press: the father aroused to see the last gasp of his dying child, as it lay in its cradle, weltering in its blood; and the husband awakened from his last sleep by the shrieks of his wife as she is brained to the earth." Faced

[9] Lovejoy to the editor, August 26, 1837, *Missouri Republican,* September 1, 1837; Lovejoy to Elizabeth Lovejoy, September 5, 1837, Lovejoy, *Memoir,* pp. 232-234.

[10] William S. Lincoln, *Alton Trials: Of Winthrop S. Gilman, Who Was Indicted for the Crime of Riot* (New York, 1838), p. 77.

with such vivid prospective terrors and the present fact of economic depression (which they blamed on Lovejoy), it is not surprising that the mob destroyed the press.[11]

The ruin of the *Observer* and the extreme antipathy of a section of the public made Lovejoy only more determined in his course. The martyr spirit which through long ages had so often defied the world could be found in Lovejoy at Alton. Having endured so much, he believed now that he could endure anything; and he recalled the Scriptural promise, "As thy days, so shall thy strength be." With little delay he resumed preparations for the antislavery convention, writing to Gerrit Smith, the wealthy antislavery philanthropist of western New York, to urge him to come to Illinois to help organize antislavery sentiment before the convention met.[12]

Lovejoy's supporters in Alton convened immediately to discuss the situation created by the destruction of the press. Should they yield to public pressure and abandon their support of Lovejoy and his newspaper? Should they allow the will of the people expressed in momentary violence to overrule the fundamental law of the land? Those were questions all who shared responsibility for the *Observer* were required to face.

Although it would have been easy for them to surrender, they decided unanimously that the *Observer* must be re-established in Alton. But how this could be accomplished was another matter. Money was scarce. Not even Godfrey and Gilman, themselves nearly crushed by the Panic of 1837 and the debacle of the Illinois State Bank, could advance the ready cash for the purchase of a new press.[13]

Lovejoy decided to make a general public appeal for financial aid. If his appeal succeeded, he reasoned, it would allow the newspaper to continue; but equally important, it would also prove to his opponents in Alton that a group of substantial citizens backed the *Observer* and deplored illegal methods to destroy it. To accomplish this purpose, Lovejoy prepared an extra number of the *Observer* in the form of a letter addressed "To the Friends and Subscribers of the Alton *Ob-*

. . . . .

[11] *Ibid.*

[12] Lovejoy to Elizabeth Lovejoy, September 5, 1837, Lovejoy, *Memoir,* p. 232; Lovejoy to Gerrit Smith, September 4, 1837, Lovejoy Collection.

[13] Lovejoy, *Memoir,* p. 245.

server," and had it printed at the office of the Alton *Telegraph*. Issued in the name of "civil and religious liberty," it urged all "friends of law and order" to "let the experiment be fairly tried whether the liberty of speech and of the press is to be enjoyed in Illinois or not." The letter did not mention slavery at all; its appeal was based entirely on the defense of civil rights. If the press were not re-established, Lovejoy predicted, "mobism" would triumph.[14]

By this means Lovejoy's situation became known to abolitionists everywhere. John Rankin of New York sent him a small contribution; so did David Lee Child, one of the founders of the American Anti-Slavery Society and a close follower of Garrison. And in spite of the economic depression, most Illinois antislavery men found themselves able to contribute at least something to the cause once the implications of mob action were made clear to them. Winthrop S. Gilman, Lovejoy's earlier benefactor, managed to scrape together another $100. Soon small amounts began to trickle in from subscribers and antislavery groups in other parts of Illinois—enough to allow Lovejoy to send his brother Owen, recently arrived from Maine, to Cincinnati to purchase a third press. However, it was still necessary for Lovejoy to arrange for additional credit from the Cincinnati merchant who supplied the press and printing material.[15]

No sooner had this been accomplished than hearts in Alton grew faint. Some of those men who had thus far supported Lovejoy began to question whether the maintenance of the *Observer* as an abolitionist newspaper against such determined opposition was really worth the effort after all, whether it would not be wise to sacrifice abstract principle in the interest of social tranquillity.

No doubt such a change in attitude resulted partly from discouragement at repeated disappointments, but it was also in part the work of a newcomer to Alton. Late in the summer of 1837 the Reverend Joel Parker, a brilliant young Presbyterian preacher who would later become president of Union Theological Seminary, arrived in the city

. . . . .

[14] *Ibid.*, pp. 245-247.

[15] Lincoln, *Alton Trials*, p. 107; Lovejoy, *Memoir*, p. 246; John Rankin to Lovejoy, September 11, 1837, Aratus Kent to Lovejoy, September 6, 1837, Wickett-Wiswall Collection; Lovejoy to James G. Birney, October 7, 1837, Boston *Liberator*, November 3, 1837.

from New Orleans. Parker, about Lovejoy's age, was a rising power in the church. Like Lovejoy, he had come to the attention of powerful Presbyterian clergymen at an early age, but unlike Lovejoy, he subordinated social reform to other considerations. He opposed slavery only mildly and felt no sympathy at all for the abolitionist cause. To add to his own influence, he brought with him copies of a persuasive proslavery pamphlet written by the Reverend James Smylie of Mississippi. The Bible, Smylie's pamphlet sought to prove, did not so explicitly condemn slavery as many Northerners had been led to believe. Even if American slavery did have its bad points, Smylie suggested, it was nonetheless an institution accepted by the Prophets and a social arrangement sanctioned by Scripture. Of course this argument contained nothing new, but never before had it been presented so convincingly in Alton and at a time when so many were anxious to adopt any logic that might produce peace.[16]

While Smylie's pamphlet whittled away at the abolitionist argument, extreme conservatives in the city revived the local branch of the American Colonization Society as an alternative means of dealing with the slavery problem. Many people seized upon its program of sending freed slaves to Africa as both a happy solution to the racial problem and a means of avoiding the moral decisions the abolitionists asked them to make.[17]

Thus just as Lovejoy was preparing to re-establish the *Observer* at the end of September, a serious lack of unity appeared among its supporters. The influence of Smylie's pamphlet and of the American Colonization Society had weakened the determination of some of the former defenders of the press. Their wavering, in turn, had helped to confirm Lovejoy's opponents in their hostility toward him. Some decided that if the *Observer* continued publication at all, it ought to alter its character and become a strictly religious paper, meddling no more with subjects in any sense tangential to theology. Some concluded that the only proper course was to find a new editor.[18]

Lovejoy himself gave little thought to the danger the changing situ-

. . . . .

[16] Lovejoy, *Memoir*, p. 247; James Smylie, *A Review of a Letter, from the Presbytery of Mississippi, on the Subject of Slavery* (Woodville, Mississippi, 1836).

[17] Alton *Telegraph*, July 19, 1836; Beecher, *Narrative*, pp. 41-44.

[18] Lovejoy, *Memoir*, pp. 247-248.

ation created, but other abolitionists did. The division of opinion in Alton, his friends realized, could easily prove fatal to their cause. If those who had previously defended the paper were seen to waver in its support, its opponents would be only the more determined to silence it permanently. Aware of this possibility, Winthrop S. Gilman proposed to Lovejoy that before trying to establish a third press in Alton he give some evidence to the public that respectable men throughout the state had resolved to support its legal right to operate. Only in such a way, Gilman thought, could the mob be intimidated. Accordingly, Gilman drew up a statement pledging all who signed it to maintain the supremacy of the law in Illinois, and Lovejoy sent copies to his friends to be circulated in Quincy, Jacksonville, and Springfield. "Forward it to me, *as soon as possible*," he urged. "Take some pains to get signers as extensively as possible and as speedily too."[19]

The statement Lovejoy asked to have signed made no mention of slavery, nor did it in any way express sympathy with antislavery doctrine. Its circulation, therefore, was an attempt by Lovejoy and Gilman to divorce the issue of protecting the freedom of the press from the issue of forming an antislavery society. They hoped in this way to obtain the backing of many persons who did not wish to identify themselves with the organized antislavery movement but who would rally to the defense of civil rights. A clear promise by respectable citizens to uphold the law would place the defense of the *Observer* on a basis firm enough to assure its safety in Alton.

On the same day that Lovejoy mailed this paper to antislavery men outside Alton, he himself received a personal letter from Gilman. Since drawing up the statement, Gilman had thought over once again the problems involved in maintaining the *Observer* in Alton. Overnight he had lost faith in his own plan to produce unity. The state of feeling toward the *Observer* had grown so hopelessly divided, Gilman told Lovejoy, that he had decided to give no more aid to the newspaper. And, he wrote somewhat petulantly, "I think it becomes a very serious question whether duty should not induce you to retire from it—."[20]

. . . . .

[19] W. S. Gilman to Our Fellow Citizens of the State of Illinois, September 7, 1837, Lovejoy to Erastus Wright, September 8, 1837, Elijah P. Lovejoy Papers (Illinois State Historical Library).

[20] Gilman to Lovejoy, September 8, 1837, Lovejoy Collection.

One can only imagine Lovejoy's feelings as he read Gilman's letter. If Gilman had at last deserted him, the number in Alton on whose support he could count must be limited indeed. Who were they? Frederick W. Graves, pastor of the Presbyterian church—probably. Hubbell Loomis, pastor of the Baptist church—perhaps. Maybe he could have confidence in a half-dozen other abolitionists besides, but scarcely more than ten men in the entire county were willing publicly to affirm that they would defend his right to edit his newspaper as he saw fit.[21]

The reality of the situation shook Lovejoy. For two days he tried to decide what to do. The physical welfare both of himself and of his family would certainly be improved if he left Alton. The constant strain and the social disapproval had worked a terrible hardship on Celia Lovejoy, contributing to the illness from which she now suffered constantly. Surely the test of printing an antislavery newspaper in Alton had been fairly tried. It had failed. Momentarily he wondered if Gilman were not right. Perhaps as Gilman had said, "duty" did require him to abandon his struggle to remain in Alton as editor of the *Observer*.

But Owen Lovejoy, recently arrived from Maine where he had been influenced by his abolitionist mother and brother Joseph, was not so sure that Elijah needed to take so drastic and final a step. Leave the matter entirely up to the present and former supporters of the paper, he suggested. After all, Gilman did not speak for everyone, and it might be that even his opponents would reconsider. Lovejoy yielded to Owen's argument. The result of the present crisis, he believed, would have repercussions everywhere. If he left the city, he would by that act abdicate his civil rights, abandoning a portion of them to the tyranny of a mob, and thus he would weaken individual liberty throughout the nation. Any personal sacrifice he might be required to make by remaining in Alton would be a small thing when measured against the effect his steadfastness might have on the preservation of a free press in America.[22]

He decided to present the matter to the public, as Owen suggested. On September 11 he addressed a letter to "The Friends of the Redeemer in Alton," offering to accept their verdict on the question of

. . . . .

[21] Lovejoy to Joshua Leavitt, October 3, 1837, Lovejoy, *Memoir*, p. 259.
[22] Lovejoy, *Memoir*, p. 261.

his remaining as editor of the *Observer*. Would his resignation be best "for the cause of truth; most for the glory of God, and the salvation of souls?" he asked. "Be it yours, brethren, to decide what is best, and rest assured—whatever my own private judgment may be—of my cordial acquiescence in your decision."[23]

In case they decided to change editors, he had only one request to make. The supporters of the paper should assume the debts he had incurred while running it, and, since he was nearly penniless, contribute to the cost of his moving from the city. When these terms had been met, he would submit to them the *Observer*'s subscription list of more than 2,100 names. Two thousand dollars was due from subscriptions and $350 more from job printing. But he owed $3,350, mostly to the journeymen printers, plus an indefinite amount to John Viall, the traveling agent, and to Thaddeus B. Hurlbut, the assistant editor, who so far had been paid nothing.[24]

Lovejoy's letter was less an offer to resign than an effort to shock the consciences of the men to whom it was directed, in the hope of forcing them to unite and to back him and his press. Within a few days it brought action. Fifteen men interested in the welfare of the *Observer* came to meet with Lovejoy to consider the matter. They debated two resolutions at their first meeting: (1) that the Alton *Observer* ought to be re-established; and (2) that Lovejoy ought to continue as its editor. After very little discussion everyone present agreed to the necessity of continuing the newspaper in Alton, but the second resolution brought dissent. A leading member of the Presbyterian church declared that if the *Observer* were re-established and pursued its former policy, he could not help to protect it. A prominent merchant agreed. The Reverend John Hogan, pastor of the Methodist church, said he felt the same way about it. Although they discussed the second resolution through several successive meetings, they could come to no agreement as to whether Lovejoy ought to be replaced or not. The Alton *Spectator* made its influence felt in the deliberations by repeating the old canard that Lovejoy had come to Alton to publish a religious newspaper only and had in fact pledged not to discuss abo-

. . . . .

[23] Lovejoy to the Friends of the Redeemer in Alton, September 11, 1837, Lewis Tappan Papers (Manuscript Division, Library of Congress).

[24] *Ibid.;* Statement of the *Observer*'s Affairs, September 11, 1837, Elijah P. Lovejoy Papers.

lition. His failure to keep his promise had turned Alton into an abolitionist center with consequent loss of trade and civic reputation.[25]

Meanwhile, the replies to Lovejoy's request for the names of men who would pledge themselves to maintain the law in Illinois arrived only in small numbers. This indecision and the indecision to keep Lovejoy as editor meant, in effect, that the people of Alton could not bring themselves to agree to protect Lovejoy's right to publish his views about slavery. Anyone who wished to use violence against the *Observer* or against Lovejoy's person could now feel free to do so, for no one of authority had suggested that the law would be maintained or that mobs would be put down and their leaders punished.

With excitement in Alton increasing daily, attempts were made here and there to halt the growing threat of violence, always, however, with the thought that compromise on the issues involved was possible. The Reverend James De Pui, rector of St. Paul's Episcopal Church in Alton, delivered and subsequently published a lecture counseling moderation and respect for the law. Cautiously avoiding the appearance of partiality, he was careful to condemn the policies both of the antislavery men and of those who opposed them. He suggested that good men should be neutral. But that, of course, was a part of the present difficulty: too many "good men" failed to stand on the side of law and order. De Pui's advice could hardly bring peace to Alton.[26]

With his future thus undecided, his support uncertain, Lovejoy left Alton in the middle of September to attend the commencement exercises at Illinois College. Before he had returned, the new press arrived from Cincinnati. On September 21 near sundown some of his friends received it from the steamboat and carried it to Reuben Gerry and Royal Weller's warehouse on Second Street. Although no one molested them while this was going on, they had heard rumors that a mob intended to wreck this press as they had the others. Deciding this time to make a direct appeal to the law for protection, Lovejoy's friends notified the newly elected mayor, John M. Krum, that the press had arrived and that very likely someone would try to destroy it before

. . . . .

[25] Lovejoy, *Memoir,* p. 250.

[26] James De Pui, *Evil Effects of Angry Excitement: A Sermon Delivered Before the Congregation of St. Paul's Church, Alton, Illinois, Sunday Evening, September 17, 1837* (Alton, 1837).

it could be put in operation. The twenty-seven-year-old mayor assured them he would protect the press. All that needed to be done, he promised, was to leave its security entirely in his hands.

Mayor Krum posted a constable at the door of the warehouse that night with orders to remain until eleven o'clock, when presumably everyone would be in bed and all danger past. As soon as that hour had struck, however, and the constable had gone, some twenty men broke into the building, carried the press across Second Street, and began taking it apart. Then a new arrival appeared. Someone had called the mayor, who now came hurrying to the scene. The mob must disperse, he ordered. They would disperse, they replied, as soon as they had finished. With this defiance of authority they continued the destruction while the mayor watched, and by midnight they had completed their task. Thus before the press had been in Alton six hours, the mob had broken it up, and its parts lay at the bottom of the river. The mayor, who had observed the entire proceedings, then went home. Later he was reported to have said that it had been an unusually "quiet and gentlemanly mob."[27]

A few days after this, Lovejoy returned from Jacksonville to confront the problems produced by the destruction of his third press. Before he had decided what his next step ought to be, the pastor of the Presbyterian church in St. Charles, Missouri, invited him to deliver two sermons in that city. Since he had already planned to go to St. Charles to meet his wife, who had been visiting her mother, he accepted. Unfortunately for him, on the same weekend he was in St. Charles a white woman in the city was raped by a Negro. Sentiment raged against Lovejoy. This was the sort of thing, some said, that abolitionists encouraged.[28]

On Sunday evening after he had delivered the second sermon and returned to his mother-in-law's home, several men broke into the house and attempted to drag him out into the yard, where a mob awaited. But they were hesitant and not possessed with the fury successful mobs usually feel. Lovejoy, still adhering to his policy of pacifism, did not resist his assailants. He was protected rather by the

. . . . .

[27] Alton *Telegraph,* September 27, 1837; Lovejoy, *Memoir,* pp. 250-251; Cincinnati *Philanthropist,* September 8 and 22, 1837.

[28] Lovejoy to Joshua Leavitt, October 3, 1837, Lovejoy, *Memoir,* p. 255.

pleas of his wife, her sister, and her mother, who persuaded them to abandon their efforts to capture him. Intruders entered the house four times that night, however. The third time, they ordered Lovejoy to leave St. Charles at once. He sent a note to those who remained outside assuring them that he had already taken passage on the stage and would be gone by nine o'clock the next morning. This answer did not please the mob, and a group stormed into the house again. This time, at the insistence of his family, Lovejoy left by a back door and made his way unperceived to the home of Major George Sibley, who lent him a horse. Thus able to escape, he rode away from St. Charles, arriving at the outskirts of St. Louis at daybreak. Celia Lovejoy, ill and exhausted from the tensions of the night, joined him in the morning, and they returned to Alton later that day.

Ten of Lovejoy's friends guarded his house that night, fearing the mob would pursue him to Alton. Nothing happened, however, and the second night the Lovejoy family stayed alone. While Mrs. Lovejoy remained in a nearly hysterical state, Lovejoy lay with a loaded musket at his bedside; and his brothers Owen and John sat in the next room guarding the doors with pistols and loaded muskets.[29]

The scene would have shocked a large segment of the abolitionists, for abolitionists did not ordinarily approve the use of armed resistance, preferring to rely instead on moral force to protect themselves against carnal enemies. Lovejoy had experimented with their policy. Now he abandoned it, for moral force to be effective requires a measure of public approval somewhere in the community for the man who uses it—unless, of course, he deliberately courts martyrdom. While Lovejoy was prepared for such a fate, he did not seek it. He had learned, moreover, that neither the laws nor public sentiment could be counted on to protect him and his property in Alton. Four-fifths of the inhabitants of the city, he believed, rejoiced that his press had been destroyed. Although the respectable elements professed to hate mobs, they appeared to hate abolitionists still more. The necessities of survival in a hostile society had led him to the fateful decision to accept the use of force.[30]

Such desertion by the majority caused Lovejoy neither fear nor

. . . . .

[29] *Ibid.*, pp. 251-258; Peoria *Register*, October 14, 1837.

[30] Lovejoy to Leavitt, October 3, 1837, Lovejoy, *Memoir*, pp. 258-259.

discouragement. He had learned to accept without despair or rebellion the temporary triumph of forces he believed evil, and he had reached an intellectual position where the considerations that ordinarily govern and direct men simply did not apply. "By the blessing of God," he pledged at that moment, "I will never abandon the enterprise so long as I live, and until success has crowned it. . . . And if I am to die it cannot be in a better cause." Alton had become a testing ground, he believed, not only for himself but for all Americans as well. Freedom for the unbound individual would live or die, depending on the success of his mission.[31]

Meanwhile, during his visit at Jacksonville, he had conferred with clergymen from other parts of Illinois gathered for the college commencement. To his great satisfaction he found most of them convinced that the maintenance of free discussion demanded that he continue to edit the *Observer* in Alton. Edward Beecher, president of Illinois College and one of the most respected men in the state, agreed with this view. Beecher had long resisted Lovejoy's efforts to enlist him in support of a state antislavery society. Although since 1835 Beecher had believed immediate emancipation to be the proper solution to the problem of slavery, he had joined no antislavery society, and his conservative temperament and his position as a college president had made him hesitant to speak publicly on the subject. Now, however, the principle involved in the continued peril to the *Observer* induced Beecher, if with reluctance, to participate actively in the antislavery movement.[32]

The scheduled antislavery convention, Beecher believed, ought to reflect the special need of the moment; that is, a determination by the respectable element in the state to defend the freedom of the press. In conformity with the common opinion that the real issue in Alton was civil rights, not slavery, Beecher suggested to Lovejoy that he change the character of the convention. Let it not be solely an antislavery convention, he urged, but rather a meeting open to everyone willing to support the free discussion of slavery. This would bring to Alton many influential men who would never willingly attend an antislavery convention, but who would defend the freedom of the press. A

. . . . .

[31] *Ibid.*, p. 260.
[32] Beecher, *Narrative*, p. 24.

successful convention would prove to those who had repeatedly attacked the *Observer* that public opinion was against them. Beecher and the rest of the clergymen who assembled at Jacksonville understood Lovejoy as agreeing to Beecher's proposal. On that basis, Lovejoy obtained their support for the convention.[33]

As soon as he had returned to Alton, Lovejoy issued an extra number of the *Observer* (printed by the *Telegraph*'s press) formally inviting the "friends of free inquiry" to meet in Alton on October 26. There they would discuss the best course to take regarding slavery; but, Lovejoy promised, nobody by his attendance would be committed to the project of forming an antislavery society. In addition, however, and contrary to Beecher's wishes, Lovejoy limited his invitation to those persons who believed slavery a sin which ought to be immediately abandoned. The call was endorsed by 255 signers, 23 of whom were from Alton.[34]

Beecher was so upset by this restriction on the membership that he hurried to Alton to try to persuade Lovejoy of his error. The convention, Beecher thought, must serve to unite all men in the defense of civil rights, no matter whether they believed in immediate emancipation or not. Lovejoy's insistence upon inviting only abolitionists would do nothing to promote good feeling in Alton, nothing to prevent mob action. Indeed, such a convention as Lovejoy planned would probably only aggravate an already dangerous situation.

The two men discussed the matter thoroughly in Lovejoy's home at Alton. Lovejoy, who was acquainted with conditions in Alton as Beecher was not, was convinced that the invitation must be limited in order to prevent the intrusion of persons who opposed a free discussion of slavery in any circumstance. Beecher, unable to comprehend the passions of the mob at Alton, could not believe that men who had already destroyed two presses would dare to call themselves friends of free inquiry and attend the meetings.[35]

Beecher proposed that the convention not even try to organize a

[33] *Ibid.*, pp. 24-25.

[34] Alton *Observer,* September 28, 1837, quoted in Cincinnati *Philanthropist,* October 13, 1837; a corrected list of signers is in Hermann R. Muelder, "Printer's Error in Call for Antislavery Convention," *Journal of the Illinois State Historical Society,* XLVII (Autumn, 1954), 321-323.

[35] Beecher, *Narrative,* pp. 25-26.

formal state antislavery society. Instead, he repeated, its sole purpose must be to defend civil rights. All respectable men could be persuaded to attend such a meeting, Beecher believed. The convention, if it wished, could appoint committees to investigate the various aspects of slavery and the problems involved in discussing it, but, for the present at least, all plans to organize an antislavery society ought to be deferred. Perhaps organization could come eventually, but only after civil rights had been protected and some of the hostility toward antislavery ideas had disappeared. The convention, if properly planned, would restore order to Alton. Beecher's will, with his optimistic views and his powerful intellect, prevailed. Lovejoy approved his plan as the last hope of ending the division in Alton.[36]

Lovejoy himself had aroused so much controversy that he could not serve as spokesman for those who sought to restore order. Therefore, Beecher took the first steps in the new effort to produce unity. He called a meeting of Alton's leading church members and explained to them that their own refusal to support law and order had caused mob action. Unless they now strongly backed civil rights, he warned, still more outbreaks of violence would occur. He urged all church members to attend the scheduled convention in order "that thus the partisans of violence might be rebuked by the united voice of the wise and the good." The members of the meeting, enthusiastic over this idea, approved Beecher's plan to open the convention to everyone who desired a free discussion of slavery. Beecher then left Alton and began an extensive correspondence with men throughout the state in an attempt to persuade "the wise and the good" to attend the convention.[37]

He would need to be persuasive indeed if he were to win the support of many people at Alton, for Lovejoy's former backing there had all but disappeared. Most of the leading men of the city frankly blamed him for the recurring mob action. If he would only cease antagonizing the public, they said, the wrath would subside. In this view they were of course correct, although by saying so they ignored all principles of civil rights. But legal rights and abstract theory held little appeal for them. They were more concerned about the peace of the city. Few

• • • • •

[36] *Ibid.*, p. 27.

[37] *Ibid.*, pp. 26-27.

seem to have reflected that in discussing slavery, Lovejoy was only exercising a right guaranteed him by the Constitution of the United States, and that in silencing the *Observer,* the public was doing something no Northern court could have done.

Thus deprived of the support of most of the prominent citizens of Alton, Lovejoy was left nearly alone to face the mounting wrath of the less respectable elements of the community. In other parts of the state, however, many of his friends remained loyal. The abolitionists at Quincy repeatedly urged him to remove his press to their city, where, they assured him, the public would gladly protect it. When Lovejoy attended the synod of Illinois at Springfield in the middle of October (after a public meeting in the courthouse square had threatened to prevent its assembly), he found the Presbyterian clergy ready to reaffirm their earlier stand against slavery. But even here his support was not unanimous. When Beecher introduced a resolution to put the synod on record as condemning the action of the Alton mob and assuring Lovejoy of its support, some negative votes were cast. Ignoring such opposition, the majority of the clergy at the Springfield meeting reaffirmed their "encouragement and approval" of Lovejoy and his newspaper.[38]

With this assurance that at least some prominent men in Illinois were resolved to defend his right to publish the *Observer,* Lovejoy returned to Alton to await the scheduled convention, now only a week away.

. . . . .

[38] Lovejoy, *Memoir,* pp. 261-262; Minutes of the Synod of Illinois, New School, 1831-69, I, 119-120; Beecher, *Narrative,* pp. 27-28; Historical Records Survey, Illinois, *Inventory of Church Archives: Presbyterian Church in the United States of America, Springfield Presbytery* (Chicago, 1942), p. 23; Arthur Theodore Andreas, *History of Chicago from the Earliest Period to the Present Time* (Chicago, 1885), I, 302.

Forming a State Antislavery Society

Chapter XI

Edward Beecher, busily writing letters and holding conferences to arouse interest in the forthcoming convention, had managed to take the direction of affairs out of Lovejoy's hands. Believing the convention could succeed only if it were limited to abolitionists, Lovejoy had invited only men who were convinced of the sin of slavery. Beecher now decided that his own plans to create harmony required a wider invitation.

On October 18, 1837, readers of the Alton *Telegraph* found an open letter in its columns addressed "To the Friends of Free Discussion," and signed by Beecher. Everyone interested in free speech, Beecher wrote, would be welcome at the antislavery convention in Alton on October 26. On that day, he said, men of good will from all over the state would "meet and kindly discuss, and see if there cannot be found some great principle on which all good men can unite." No force on earth could stop the discussion of a moral question so important as slavery, declared Beecher. Therefore only two alternatives remained in Alton—either unregulated controversy, destructive to the "harmony and peace of society," or a convention for peaceable discussion, such as the one he proposed.[1]

Although Lovejoy objected to none of this in theory, he suspected Beecher both of underestimating the strength of the opposition and of

. . . . .

[1] Alton *Telegraph,* October 18, 1837.

exaggerating its reasonableness. Beecher's new invitation, Lovejoy feared, would serve only to open the convention to people who had no intention of allowing antislavery ideas to circulate freely. And, in any event, he had called the convention for quite a different purpose.

The Illinois abolitionists were conscious of acting on the national stage; they knew that antislavery leaders across the nation watched their progress with the greatest concern. The American Anti-Slavery Society, anxiously awaiting the outcome of the struggle in Alton, directed its corresponding secretary to try to persuade James G. Birney, the prominent Ohio abolitionist, to visit the state before the impending convention in order to "give them the right sort of fire." The Ohio Anti-Slavery Society accepted Lovejoy's invitation to appoint delegates to attend the meeting, and abolitionists in New York and Boston sent him small financial contributions. Eastern abolitionists in no sense minimized the significance of the West to the antislavery movement. Illinois was "the seat of war," wrote Joshua Leavitt, editor of the New York *Emancipator,* and the antislavery leaders in the East were "mere powder monkeys" supplying ammunition for the crucial battle being fought in the West.[2]

Lovejoy, now the "most interesting object in the anti-slavery ranks" (as Garrison had lately observed), expected to use the proposed convention to further the abolitionist cause in the United States. The convention, he hoped, would form a state-wide antislavery society for the purpose of spreading antislavery doctrine and winning more converts to the movement. Since Beecher was proposing something altogether different, Lovejoy and most other abolitionists could not concur with him in either his plans or his premises.[3]

They saw no real distinction, as Beeecher did, between the natural rights they hoped to restore to the slave and the civil rights they hoped to preserve for themselves. Neither were they under any illusions that they could ever persuade the majority in Alton to let them carry out their projects unhampered. Beecher's "great principle" of unity, they suspected, would never be fulfilled. Unlike more experienced aboli-

. . . . .

[2] Elizur Wright, Jr., to James G. Birney, August 14, 1837, Dumond (ed.), *Birney Letters,* I, 414; Lovejoy to Birney, October 7, 1837, Boston *Liberator,* November 3, 1837; Leavitt to Asa Hale, quoted in Hale to Asa Turner, January 26, 1838, in private possession of Mrs. Jessie L. T. Cordiner, Alhambra, California.

[3] Boston *Liberator,* October 20, 1837.

tionists, Beecher still believed that the questions of slavery and civil rights could be separated. He did not yet share Lovejoy's knowledge that most men in Alton who were unwilling to admit the sin of slavery were also unwilling to allow the discussion of the sin of slavery to continue.

By 1837 few abolitionists in the United States were any longer interested in reaching a compromise with anyone who refused to accept both the idea of the sinfulness of slavery and the necessity for its immediate abandonment. Yet it was toward compromise that Beecher's proposals would lead. The intellectual position of the abolitionists afforded them no room for retreat, and it was expecting too much to suppose that men who hated antislavery ideas enough to allow three printing presses to be wrecked would themselves yield.

To Beecher, the principle immediately at stake in Illinois seemed to be whether or not a mob could destroy the right of free inquiry and free discussion. For the preservation of these basic civil rights, he was prepared to forego antislavery organization. This does not mean that Beecher neglected the principles involved in the antislavery movement; rather, it means that to him nothing else but principle mattered. If to maintain the right of free discussion, which was immediately at stake in Alton, something less essential must be abandoned, then so it must be. But he made a distinction most abolitionists could not see; and he anticipated a compromise few were willing to make.

Beecher himself soon realized that the opponents of abolition had responded to his invitation with something less than enthusiasm. Two days before the convention was scheduled to begin, the Alton Colonization Society met once again. This could only mean that its leaders had in no way changed their minds. The proceedings of their meeting proved that the division of opinion in Alton had in no way abated, that many important citizens still so intensely hated the idea of abolishing slavery that they could not talk about it without arousing prejudice against abolitionists. When Beecher received news of the meeting, he began to doubt the wisdom of his invitation to the "friends of free discussion," but by that time it seemed too late to do anything about it.[4]

. . . . .

[4] Alton *Telegraph,* November 1 and 22, 1837; Alton *Western Pioneer,* October 27, 1837; Lovejoy, *Memoir,* pp. 262-263.

On the afternoon of October 26, the antislavery convention met as scheduled in the Presbyterian church at Upper Alton. For several days abolitionists from all parts of Illinois had been arriving in town, prepared to help organize a state society and to support Lovejoy and his press. At Lovejoy's invitation, the Ohio State Anti-Slavery Society had sent two delegates to help with the proceedings. Most of the other eighty-five members of the convention were Presbyterian and Congregational clergymen who believed slavery a sin and freedom of inquiry a sacred right. Now they had come to Alton prepared to defend and further those ideas.

It was a colorful and in many respects a distinguished gathering, with even a sprinkling of members closely associated with the national antislavery movement. Lovejoy, of course, was the most prominent abolitionist present, but others possessed a longer record in the movement than he. The large delegation from Galesburg included the Reverend John J. Miter, whose experience in the antislavery movement exceeded that of any other man in Illinois. After studying at Oneida Seminary in western New York when Charles G. Finney had conducted his great revivals there, Miter had moved to Lane Seminary with the group led by Theodore Weld. At Lane he had participated in the antislavery debates that convulsed the institution in 1834, and subsequently, as one of the "Lane rebels," he had traveled widely as a lecturer for the American Anti-Slavery Society.[5]

From Carlinville in Macoupin County came two neighbors, Gideon Blackburn and James M. Buchanan, both recent emigrants from Kentucky and close friends of James G. Birney, who edited the antislavery *Philanthropist* in Cincinnati. Blackburn, an old man now, had moved to Illinois in order to rear his orphaned grandchildren in a free state after a career of great distinction in the South. Buchanan, formerly a faculty member at Centre College, of which Blackburn had been president, had served as the first president of the Kentucky Anti-Slavery Society.[6]

. . . . .

[5] Barnes and Dumond (eds.), *Weld-Grimké Letters,* I, 83n.

[6] James M. Buchanan to James G. Birney, Dumond (ed.), *Birney Letters,* I, 416; Blackburn to Absalom Peters, April 12, May 22, 1833, AHMS Papers; *Proceedings of the Kentucky Anti-Slavery Society at Its First Meeting in Danville, Ky., March 19th, 1835* (n.p., 1835).

Jeremiah Porter, Lovejoy's friend from Peoria, had come to Alton to lend the cause his support. Among other delegates from central Illinois were William Kirby, Lucien Farnham, Elisha Jenney, and Asa Turner, all former students at Yale Theological Seminary and members of the "Yale Band" who had moved to the Illinois frontier to found Illinois College.[7]

The thirty-two men attending from Alton and Madison County included Lovejoy's loyal supporter, Frederick W. Graves, Thomas Lippincott, a former Quaker whose extreme opposition to slavery dated back more than a dozen years, and Thaddeus B. Hurlbut, Lovejoy's editorial associate, whose attachment to the antislavery cause proved sufficient to lead him to name his only son Wilberforce Lovejoy Hurlbut.[8]

Alanson Work and George Thompson rode down to the convention from Quincy with David Nelson, who had helped bring Lovejoy into the antislavery movement. A few years later, Work and Thompson would be convicted of helping slaves escape from Missouri and for that offense would spend four years in jail at Palmyra, Missouri.[9]

All in all, it was an impressive group made up of men of learning and piety and dedication, but the men of affairs whom Beecher had counted on for support were not present, nor had they given any sign that they intended to come to the aid of free speech.

When Lovejoy and the other abolitionists filed into the church, prepared for the work ahead, they were shocked to see men arriving and taking seats who had never been identified with the antislavery movement or with the defense of civil rights, who were, indeed, known to have opposed Lovejoy and the *Observer*. Yet there they were: Colonel Alexander Botkin, leader of the July Market House meetings; Dr. B. K. Hart; John Hogan, who was simultaneously a wealthy whole-

. . . . .

[7] Rammelkamp, *Illinois College*, pp. 17-25; Frederick Kuhns to the Editor, *Journal of the Illinois State Historical Society*, XXXVIII (1945), 113.

[8] Edwardsville *Spectator*, November 9, 1824; A. L. Bowen, "Anti-Slavery Convention Held in Alton, Illinois, October 26-28, 1837," *Journal of the Illinois State Historical Society*, XX (1927-28), 335.

[9] Alton *Observer*, June 1, 1837; George Thompson, *Prison Life and Reflections* (Hartford, Connecticut, 1849); *Narrative of Facts Respecting Alanson Work, Jas. E. Burr, and Geo. Thompson, Prisoners in the Missouri Penitentiary* (Quincy, Illinois, 1842).

sale grocer, president of the Alton branch of the state bank, vice-president of the Alton Colonization Society, state representative from Madison County, and a Methodist preacher; William M. Carr, one of Lovejoy's most extreme opponents who was willing even to use violence against him; and dominating them all, Usher F. Linder from Kentucky, the brilliant young lawyer, not yet thirty years old, who had recently become attorney general of Illinois.[10]

If there had been a *Who's Who in Illinois* in 1837, Hogan and Linder would have been in it. Young, rich, and ambitious, they stood at the threshold of what they hoped would be great political careers in the Democratic party. Their future clearly depended on pleasing the people. The people opposed abolition; therefore, they would lead the movement to put it down. That was the main reason they had come to sit in the Prebysterian church that autumn afternoon.

At two o'clock Lovejoy rose to call the convention to order. As he looked into the faces of such men as Botkin, Hart, Hogan, and Linder, he hoped that they were sincere in attending as "friends of free discussion," but nothing in their recent records could make him believe so. He looked around the hall for Edward Beecher, who, more than anyone else, was responsible for the present situation, but he was not there. Evidently the stage bringing him from Jacksonville had been delayed. Business would have to proceed without him.[11]

Lovejoy started the meeting by calling the venerable Gideon Blackburn to the chair to preside as temporary chairman. No one, abolitionist or not, could plausibly object to the choice of Blackburn, whose opposition to slavery was well known but who had never closely identified himself with the organized antislavery movement. But when someone moved to appoint Lovejoy's close friend and fellow abolitionist, Frederick W. Graves, as temporary secretary, the "friends of free discussion" loudly protested the choice and precipitated a disorderly debate that was to continue all afternoon.

Losing patience with this obstruction to the proceeedings, Lovejoy declared that the meeting had been called by abolitionists to discuss slavery. No one, he insisted, who did not agree with abolitionist views

. . . . .

[10] *Dictionary of American Biography*, IX, 119-120; Usher F. Linder, *Reminiscences of the Early Bench and Bar of Illinois* (Chicago, 1879), p. 39.

[11] Beecher, *Narrative*, p. 28.

had any right to a seat, regardless of any gratuitous invitation Beecher might have issued.

Will you "as gentlemen," he chided, "come in and interrupt a meeting called for a specific purpose?" Their conduct so far, he pointed out, indicated that they had entered the building not to maintain the cause of free inquiry but deliberately to interrupt the convention and thwart its designs.[12]

Lovejoy's comments incensed Linder, Hogan, and Botkin. One after another they jumped up to protest with angry words and gestures this effort to limit their part in the meeting. They had been invited to attend by Edward Beecher through his letter in the *Telegraph,* they insisted, and they had responded in good faith as "friends of free discussion." Let the calls for the meeting be read. Then, they said, let it be determined whether or not all men present fitted the specifications.

While the temporary chairman read both Lovejoy's original invitation to the abolitionists and Beecher's later invitation to the "friends," Beecher himself entered the church. He realized at once that "the wise and the good" were not present; such leaders as Winthrop S. Gilman and Benjamin Godfrey, for example, on whom he had counted to support the abolitionists and to serve as counterweights to such men as Linder, had failed to attend.

Lovejoy left his seat to join Beecher, and while the debate continued, he explained the situation. Beecher quickly made up his mind what to do. Getting the floor, he renounced the invitation he had extended. He had been out of order in issuing it, he confessed; and the men who had attended on the strength of it had no right to overrule the will of the majority who had signed Lovejoy's original call to the abolitionists. The convention must be organized, he said, by first enrolling those men who believed slavery a sin. After that had been accomplished, the abolitionists could then seat such others as they pleased.[13]

Linder stood up and with the ingratiating courtroom poise for which he was famous announced that he could respond to the original

. . . . .

[12] *Ibid.,* p. 29; Lovejoy, *Memoir,* p. 265; Alton *Observer—Extra: Proceedings of the Illinois Anti-Slavery Convention Held at Upper Alton on the Twenty-sixth, Twenty-seventh, and Twenty-eighth of October, 1837* (Alton, 1838), p. 3.

[13] Beecher, *Narrative,* p. 29.

call. He, too, believed slavery a sin, he said, and wished to discuss the subject fairly and reasonably. The leader having spoken, others most unexpectedly agreed with him, claiming in that manner a right to a seat in the convention. By now it was late afternoon. The debate had been long and weary and profitless. Since nothing more could be accomplished, and both sides needed time to decide on further action, Blackburn adjourned the meeting until the next morning at nine o'clock.[14]

While the delegates were leaving the hall, Linder climbed onto a pile of wood in the churchyard and began an extemporaneous address to his followers gathered around him. The antislavery men, who talk so much about rights, he declared, tried a moment ago to deny a portion of the citizens the right of free inquiry. Such men are dangerous to the country, for they carry on their agitation unmindful of the public good (this, of course, was an echo of Judge Lawless' earlier remarks against the abolitionists). By pursuing their antislavery policy, they are driving a deep wedge between the sections. Besides, he continued, they have many strange and radical ideas about racial equality. Like all the other fanatical, meddlesome reformers spawned by New England, they only make trouble and contribute nothing to society. But don't be afraid of them, he added. They can be managed. Just come back early tomorrow morning and bring some friends with you to fill the church building.[15]

Friday morning at nine o'clock, both sides returned to the church prepared for a showdown battle for control of the convention. Linder had recruited additional dozens of men to attend the meeting as "friends of free discussion." Lovejoy and the other abolitionists had decided to organize the convention as Beecher suggested, admitting first all who could subscribe to the original call, and then voting to admit such other persons as seemed sincere in wanting a free and fair discussion of slavery.

Gideon Blackburn opened the meeting by declaring the entire proceedings of the previous afternoon out of order. The convention

. . . . .

[14] *Ibid.*, p. 30; Lovejoy, *Memoir,* p. 265; Alton *Observer–Extra,* p. 3; John J. Miter to H. B. Stanton, October 30, 1837, Boston *Liberator,* December 22, 1837.

[15] Henry Tanner, *The Martyrdom of Lovejoy. An Account of the Life, Trials, and Perils of Elijah P. Lovejoy* (Chicago, 1881), p. 220; Beecher, *Narrative,* p. 30.

would start afresh, he ruled, with the reading of Lovejoy's original call to the abolitionists, followed by an invitation for all to sign it whose consciences allowed them to do so. Then that group would vote on the question of admitting other "friends."

If the abolitionists really believed this tactic would thwart their opposition, they were much mistaken. Hogan, Linder, and most of those they had brought to the meeting took their places in line along with men like David Nelson, Elijah Lovejoy, and John Miter to sign their names to the original call.[16]

Blackburn then read a letter just handed him from the trustees of the church. Fearing violence to church property, the trustees had ruled the convention could continue to meet in the building only if all "friends of free discussion" were admitted. Colonel Botkin moved the adoption of the letter. Thus an important obstacle to control of the convention by Linder's men had been removed.[17]

With so much maneuvering out of the way, the delegates could now organize and at least make an effort to carry on business. The abolitionists nominated Blackburn for permanent chairman; their opponents picked Dr. Thomas M. Hope. Perhaps because of his known conservative position on slavery, Blackburn won easily, garnering even some of the antiabolitionists' votes. "He is as wary in relation to slavery as an old bear is of a trap," his abolitionist neighbor, James Buchanan, had said. The antislavery men were able to elect their candidate, Frederick W. Graves, for secretary, too; but by the time the third officer, another secretary, was chosen, they were outvoted, and William M. Carr received the post. All the time the elections had been going on, more of the "friends" had been entering the church; now the abolitionists found themselves in a minority.[18]

The convention participants, finally organized, could at last begin working. Amidst these proceedings Lovejoy himself, although the cause of the activity, sank temporarily into the background while others conducted the convention's business. Blackburn appointed Edward Beecher, Asa Turner, and Usher F. Linder to draw up a report of sen-

. . . . .

[16] Alton *Observer—Extra,* pp. 3-7; Beecher, *Narrative,* p. 31.

[17] Alton *Observer—Extra,* pp. 7-8.

[18] *Ibid.*; Buchanan to Birney, August 18, 1837, Dumond (ed.), *Birney Letters,* I, 416-417; Tanner, *Martyrdom,* pp. 220-221.

timents for the assembly to debate during the afternoon. The convention then adjourned while those three men, so different in background and point of view, withdrew to hammer out a statement on civil rights and slavery.

It would have been difficult to select a less harmonious committee. Both Beecher and Turner, like Lovejoy, were Eastern-born clergymen reared in New England homes and imbued with the conviction that this is a moral universe directed by God toward a predetermined end. It was their sacred duty, they believed, to cooperate with God in removing sin and moral corruption from the world. Linder, on the other hand, shared few of their values. Ambitious for political office and concerned for his own material success in this world, he paid little heed to moral law. He was convinced that whatever the people wanted they must have, that the will of the majority must rule.

Naturally, the three could agree on no statement to present to the convention. Yesterday, as Beecher reminded him, Linder had declared he believed slavery a sin. Today in the committee room he repudiated that belief. Beecher and Turner drafted resolutions defending civil rights which they copied directly from the constitution of Illinois. Linder, the attorney general of the state, refused to accept them. Instead, he insisted upon preparing his own report, which turned out to be a complete acceptance of the Southern claims in defense of slavery. According to Linder Congress had no power to abolish slavery anywhere; no state—not even a slave state—could tamper with the institution. Slavery was a "political evil" for which the present generation could not be held responsible. Free Negroes ought not to have the same rights as other free citizens; and antislavery efforts which upset "the feelings and safety of our slave-holding brethren . . . ought to be discountenanced by an intelligent community."[19]

The three men agreed on only one thing. They would present the two sets of resolutions as one report, hoping in this way that a debate on each statement would allow each side to present its views on the whole subject. It did not turn out that way. When the convention met once more on Friday afternoon, the church was full. The entire population of Alton, so it seemed, had assembled to watch the pro-

. . . . .

[19] Beecher, *Narrative,* p. 32; Alton *Observer—Extra,* pp. 8-9.

ceedings which would probably play a major part in determining Lovejoy's fate. Every seat had been taken, men were jammed in the aisles, others who could not get inside crowded around the open doors. The abolitionists had clearly been overwhelmed by their opponents. But, nonetheless, the proceedings had to continue. Beecher presented the resolutions for the committee, indicating as he did so which items had been approved by Linder alone. The convention, completely dominated by Linder's men, promptly went into the committee of the whole, discussed only one resolution (that not even the slave states possessed the right to abolish slavery), and then in rapid succession accepted it, moved the adoption of the remainder of Linder's resolutions without further debate, and adjourned sine die.[20]

Lovejoy could scarcely have suffered a greater defeat. Men prominent in politics had been willing to organize large numbers of people to oppose his plans. They had turned the convention into a farce, allowing neither the organization of a state antislavery society nor the free discussion of slavery itself. Still more important, they had proved that the abolitionists could command no effective following in Alton and that power obviously lay with their opponents. Lovejoy's position in Alton had been rendered practically untenable.

Beecher, Lovejoy, and Buchanan thought of calling another meeting later that same day to try again to organize a society, but rejected the idea as an invitation to mob action. Instead, the opponents of slavery who stayed in town met that night in small groups throughout Alton. Since most of them were members of the clergy and all of them religious men, they spent the evening in prayer, asking for divine counsel in carrying out their abused work.[21]

Out of that night of contemplation came plans to meet privately the next day to form a state antislavery society. One of the antislavery group, more cautious than the rest, suggested deferring organization in view of the formidable opposition such action was certain to arouse. Almost unanimously the suggestion was rejected. Halfway measures no longer seemed acceptable. Shocked by what appeared to them to be the tyranny of unmoral popular will, the antislavery leaders had de-

. . . . .

[20] Lovejoy, *Memoir*, p. 266; Alton *Observer—Extra*, p. 9; Miter to Stanton, October 30, 1837, Boston *Liberator*, December 22, 1837.

[21] Beecher, *Narrative*, p. 34.

cided that any kind of compromise would be fruitless. Failure to take action would be to accept a diminution of their own freedom and to hand victory to the opposition, thus making the task of antislavery men all over the nation so much the more difficult. Linder's conduct had satisfied them that organization was imperative.

The seventy-five abolitionists who remained in Alton met Saturday morning in Thaddeus B. Hurlbut's spacious two-family stone house in Upper Alton. While a mob organized by Linder surged around the house and its members beat against the doors, the abolitionists inside prayed for the success of their undertaking. Not until the mayor had sworn in forty special constables to clear the streets could the meeting proceed.[22]

With order restored, the Reverend Asa Turner took the chair. Organization, everyone agreed, had been determined a necessity. Even Beecher, who was constantly aware of the injury his association with an antislavery society would probably cause Illinois College, now declared he would join the new society. After the events of the preceding two days, he explained, "I felt it to be my imperious and solemn duty to associate myself with the injured and oppressed; and to exert whatever of influence I could exert, in maintaining their rights."[23]

The abolitionists elected Elihu Wolcott of Jacksonville as president of the new society, Elijah Lovejoy corresponding secretary, and Thaddeus Hurlbut recording secretary. Near the conclusion of the meeting, Beecher, Wolcott, and William Carter prepared a message addressed "To the Citizens of Illinois," explaining the reasons for founding the new society and the absolute certainty of its ultimate success.

The abolitionists were riding on the swiftly moving tide of history, they suggested, and to oppose them was to oppose the inevitable. Slavery, they declared, would certainly be ended soon. "No one who believes in the justice of God, and in his purpose speedily to renovate the world, can doubt that he will terminate slavery, and that ere long. . . . On this subject to be ignorant or indifferent is a crime. Every man is bound to know the truth and to exert his influence in its behalf." . . . . .

[22] *Ibid.*, pp. 34-36; Lovejoy to Birney, November, 1837, Cincinnati *Philanthropist,* November 28, 1837; Mrs. T. B. Hurlbut to Irene B. Allan, May 23, 1844, Chicago *Western Citizen,* August 8, 1844.

[23] Beecher, *Narrative,* p. 37.

And, continued the committee, let no one entertain the idea that the abolitionists will retreat before the forces of opposition, no matter how formidable. "God will no more suspend the great law of moral influence than the law of gravitation. It is his great moral power. What if men are excited and react? So did they at the gospel."[24]

In forming a state antislavery society, the convention had carried out only one of its aims. It had still to decide what to do about the *Observer*. Some practical delegates, overawed by the opposition they had encountered in Alton, thought Lovejoy ought to move the newspaper to Quincy, where they believed the community would prove friendlier. Lovejoy did not agree, however, nor did David Nelson. The piety of Adams County, Nelson had written, was much overestimated. Although "a few Congregationalists from New England are intelligent & lovely," he explained, "others in crowds are as if the nations were boiled, & the Scum thrown to one place."[25]

There was a matter of principle involved as well. As Lovejoy pointed out, if the *Observer* could be driven from one city, it could be driven from any other. It must remain in Alton, or freedom of the press would be abandoned altogether. Dr. Archibald and M. L. Brooks, attending the convention as representatives of the Ohio State Anti-Slavery Society, agreed with Nelson and Lovejoy. A retreat to Quincy, they warned, would weaken the antislavery cause throughout the country and might even prove fatal to the movement in Illinois. The continued publication of James G. Birney's *Philanthropist* in Cincinnati after a mob had attacked it in 1836 had strengthened civil rights in Ohio, they reported.[26]

These arguments sounded reasonable to the members of the convention. Before they adjourned, they decided to make still another attempt to re-establish the *Observer* in Alton with Lovejoy as editor, and they resolved this time "to take such measures as shall secure its re-establishment and safety."[27]

Events now hurried toward a final crisis. The lines were sharply

. . . . .

[24] *Ibid.*, pp. 38-40; Alton *Observer—Extra,* pp. 13-26.

[25] Beecher, *Narrative,* p. 45; Lovejoy, *Memoir,* p. 267; Nelson to Absalom Peters, June 13, 1837, AHMS Papers.

[26] Beecher, *Narrative,* p. 45; Betty Fladeland, *James Gillespie Birney: Slaveholder to Abolitionist* (Ithaca, New York, 1955), pp. 140-143.

[27] Alton *Observer—Extra,* p. 11.

drawn, the issues clear. Men of great prestige in the community had proved they would not tolerate the publication of abolitionist doctrine among them, and they had demonstrated that they could organize the support of many ordinary citizens for their stand. The abolitionist leaders, on the other hand, confident that they acted in accordance with the will of God, were resolved to continue such publication and to secure its safety. Having gone so far, both sides awaited the imminent arrival of Lovejoy's fourth printing press, which at that moment was being prepared in Cincinnati for shipment on a steamboat bound for Alton.[28]

. . . . .

[28] This press was purchased on credit. J. A. James to T. B. Hurlbut, October 30, 1837 (Illinois State Historical Library).

Defeat for Moral Reform

Chapter XII

The convention's decision to keep the antislavery press in Alton made it all the more essential to rally the neutral faction to Lovejoy's support. But how this could be done was by no means clear, although Edward Beecher thought he knew the answer. To Beecher, principle meant everything, and he supposed that others were like himself—rational, moral, willing always to sacrifice expediency to principle. He could not give up the idea that if "the wise and the good" were once told of the importance of maintaining civil rights they would rush to defend them. He remained in Alton as a guest in the home of Elijah and Celia Lovejoy, waiting for an occasion to sway public opinion. It soon came. With views at once noble and unrealistic Beecher accepted the new antislavery society's invitation to deliver two public sermons on slavery. This would be an excellent opportunity, he believed, to inform the public about facts and correct principles.[1]

After obtaining permission from the church trustees, he preached in Alton's two Presbyterian churches on Sunday, October 29, 1837. He told the congregations something about the sinfulness of slavery, but he stressed particularly "the safety of free and full inquiry, and the danger of allowing the progress of discussion to be arrested by force." To his great satisfaction the audiences seemed to be impressed with his arguments. The favorable reception encouraged him and led him

. . . . .

[1] John J. Miter to Henry B. Stanton, October 30, 1837, Boston *Liberator*, December 22, 1837.

to suppose there was hope that peace at last had come to reign at Alton.[2]

Beecher's efforts reveal the new situation in the city. With the meeting of the antislavery convention, Lovejoy had lost control of events. Having taken a stand, he became the figure about which the opposing forces swirled, leaving him, however, unmoved. Since he had himself reached an ultimate, unchangeable position, action was left to others. Consequently, events in Alton after the organization of the state antislavery society appeared to be dominated not by Lovejoy but by his friends and his enemies. The chief actors in the ensuing drama must have kept Lovejoy constantly in the foreground of their minds, for all their decisions were inevitably conditioned by the overwhelming fact of his presence. Nonetheless, Lovejoy himself no longer initiated action. He had become a catalytic agent, affecting others while remaining unchanged himself.

At the moment, Beecher was directing events, taking the steps that he hoped would move public opinion into the desired channels. The day after his antislavery sermons a delegation representing the neutral element in the city invited him to attend a public meeting that evening to discuss the crisis in Alton. Although few who would be there were abolitionists, they admitted, all of them believed the law must be upheld. They hoped Lovejoy would attend, Dr. Miles had already accepted, and they especially wanted Beecher to be present. Since this would provide just the opportunity Beecher had been looking for, he dropped his plans to return to Jacksonville and decided to remain in Alton.[3]

During the past few days Beecher had spent many hours thinking about the situation in Alton. According to his analysis the city's population was divided into three groups: a few abolitionists determined to maintain and defend Lovejoy's press; a relatively small group bent on preventing the re-establishment of the press; and between these two, the large number of neutrals who held the balance of power. Beecher's goal was to win for the abolitionists the support of the neutral force. All that needed to be done to accomplish this, he reasoned, was to present the facts to the uncommitted. After all, hadn't Americans been assured

. . . . .

[2] Beecher, *Narrative,* pp. 45-46.
[3] *Ibid.,* p. 46.

by high authority that in any fair contest truth is bound to defeat error?[4]

That evening, October 30, a group of "the wise and the good" gathered in the store of Alexander and Company in an attempt to find some way to keep the peace in Alton. Although Lovejoy attended, Beecher dominated the discussion, both because the others present deferred to his leadership as a college president and because of his own energy which grew out of his view that the occasion presented an opportunity he might never again have to influence the city's neutrals. His aim, as he began addressing the solid citizens who had gathered to hear him, was to establish in their minds the importance, even the sanctity, of the principle of free inquiry.

Erroneous ideas may be properly suppressed only by law or by argument, Beecher told the audience; it is useless and criminal to try to suppress them by force. To fail to protect men who utter unpopular ideas implies either a consciousness of error on one's own part or a distrust "of the power of God and the truth to defeat error in free discussion." To allow a mob to destroy a public newspaper, as had been done repeatedly in Alton, was a surrender of "our civil government and of all religious toleration." This was not a matter of interest solely to the citizens of Alton, insisted Beecher. Civil rights were endangered everywhere, and whatever happened in their own community would go far toward determining whether free speech and a free press would survive in America. Alton, he declared, now "stood in the very Thermopylae of the war." What Beecher was trying to do was to persuade the men sitting in Alexander and Company's store that their religious and patriotic obligation to defend the freedom of the press was compelling enough to overrule any personal objections they might have to Lovejoy or to his newspaper.[5]

The audience, however, failed to be impressed by Beecher's argument. Perhaps he had spoken on too elevated a plane, or perhaps they simply refused to accept any appeal based on something other than their immediate interests. In any event, "the wise and the good" did not accept his ideas. When he had finished speaking, they began asking

. . . . .

[4] *Ibid.*, pp. 50-51.

[5] Miter to Stanton, October 30, 1837, Boston *Liberator,* December 22, 1837; Beecher, *Narrative,* pp. 46-47.

him questions. All this theory was good enough, someone said, but wasn't it true that Lovejoy had broken his pledge not to print abolitionist material in the *Observer*? This question was obviously Lovejoy's to answer, and he stepped quietly to the front of the room to address the meeting. Although he had answered the question many times before, he patiently explained the whole thing again. He had indeed declared when he first arrived in Alton that he did not intend to discuss slavery so much as in the past, but he had also specifically stated that he did not admit the right of the public to determine what he should print, and, more than that, he had expressly reserved the right to change his mind at any time.[6]

Several others confirmed that this was exactly the way they remembered Lovejoy's statement at the meeting in July, 1836. The questioners, however, remained unsatisfied. In view of the enormous popular antipathy to abolition, someone asked, how would it be possible to maintain Lovejoy and the *Observer* in Alton, no matter how important the principle might be? The duty of civil leaders required them ultimately to sustain the law by force, Beecher replied. He advised that they defend the press and do so under the civil authorities.

But wasn't Lovejoy duty-bound to leave Alton? Didn't the Scriptures counsel that when you are persecuted in one city you should flee to another? It was Hogan speaking, in an attempt to warp the force of religious obligation and turn it against Lovejoy.

It may be that men have such a responsibility when the government persecutes, Beecher answered. But, he continued, the government in Alton had not persecuted Lovejoy; in fact, it had failed to use its authority in any respect during this crisis. Government, Beecher insisted, should use its power positively to enforce the laws. It had not yet done so in Alton.

The last questioner had touched upon the main issue as Beecher and Lovejoy saw it. Had things come to such a pass in Alton that the civil authorities would deny protection to a law-abiding American citizen? Beecher insisted that if the leading men present at that moment would put pressure on the government and on the mob, order would be restored immediately. Apparently he convinced some of

. . . . .

[6] Beecher, *Narrative*, p. 47.

them that this was their duty, although no formal action of any kind was taken that evening.[7]

As Lovejoy and Beecher left Alexander and Company's store after the meeting, they realized that they had probably not won the support of enough people to intimidate the mob. They could be sure of only one thing—very few men in Alton were determined to defend the press by force. Accordingly, the two decided to visit the mayor and seek his aid and direction. Mayor Krum appeared sympathetic. Although he was by no means an abolitionist, he had been elected to his office only two months earlier and was anxious for his administration to succeed. Therefore, he consented to organize a regular company of city guard to act under his authority for the maintenance of the law. Unfortunately for the peace and quiet of the city, he never got around to forming the company.[8]

That same evening, Beecher preached another sermon on slavery. This time he discussed the plan of immediate abolition, trying to show that it was neither a radical nor an impractical idea, and that no division needed to exist between the colonization and antislavery societies. His reasoning on this topic was considered to be unusually persuasive, and since only a few had attended the service, the abolitionists decided to invite him to repeat his arguments on Wednesday evening in the Presbyterian church in Upper Alton, where Lovejoy had served that summer as pastor. Before the sermon they posted placards along the streets of Alton announcing the event. However good their intentions, this act could only be considered by the opponents of abolition as a deliberate affront and a challenge.[9]

Accepting the challenge, the Alton Colonization Society met the night before the scheduled sermon. As usual, its proceedings were directed more against abolitionists than against slavery. The featured speaker of the evening, the Reverend Joel Parker, who had preached for nearly four years in New Orleans, declared it an un-Christian act to enter a community and promulgate doctrines calculated to disturb and agitate the populace—a reference that might be taken to apply to

. . . . .

[7] *Ibid.*, pp. 47-49.

[8] *Ibid.*, p. 49.

[9] *Ibid.*, pp. 49-50; Henry Tanner, *History of the Rise and Progress of the Alton Riots* (Buffalo, New York, 1878), p. 8; Lincoln, *Alton Trials*, p. 73.

both Beecher and Lovejoy and certainly to the scheduled abolitionist sermon.[10]

The next day as the hour for Beecher's address drew near, rumors flew about the city that a mob planned to disrupt the service. Winthrop S. Gilman, growing anxious both for the safety of his friends and for the safety of the church building, urged the mayor to attend the meeting and aid in keeping order. For some time Gilman, like Lovejoy and Beecher, had been pondering the advisability of defending abolitionist interests by force, since the city government appeared altogether lacking in initiative. Now he asked the mayor what he thought about placing firearms near the church in case violence should actually be attempted. Although the mayor doubted that there would be any disturbance, he did agree that it would be wise to have arms at some convenient place should they be needed, and he agreed to humor Gilman, Alton's leading citizen, by attending the service.[11]

Lovejoy remained at home while Beecher spoke that night to a large congregation, some of whom, it is safe to say, had been attracted as much by the promise of excitement as by the desire to learn more about abolitionist doctrine. The antislavery men had made careful preparations to maintain order. Guns had been carried to the house next door, and men were posted on the church balcony to defend Beecher. The prayers and the sermon proceeded with no interruption, however. But toward the end of the service, just when everyone had concluded all would be well, a stone sailed through the west window between Beecher and the audience. Someone in the balcony cried "to arms," and the guards rushed to the house next door to pick up their weapons. While Beecher finished his sermon, guards stood in line in the vestibule with their weapons in their hands. As the congregation left the church, they were met by a disorderly crowd, many of them half-grown boys, some throwing stones and shouting "coward" at the armed guards. No serious clashes took place, however; the mayor ordered everyone to leave; and relative order was maintained. Beecher could return to the Lovejoy home to report to his host that the main

. . . . .

[10] Lovejoy, *Memoir,* p. 267.

[11] Lincoln, *Alton Trials,* p. 37.

force of the mob had apparently not thought it worthwhile to stifle Beecher. They would save their efforts for the press.[12]

Excitement in Alton became almost unbearable as the hours passed, and then the days, and still the press did not arrive. Every boat that landed was met by both those who would protect the press and those who would destroy it. Grim-faced, determined men boarded each vessel as it docked, sometimes quarreling with passengers and threatening to throw overboard any boxes they suspected of holding the press. "There is So Much Excitement in our Place on The Subject of Abalishionism that realy I am Confused," wrote Benjamin Godfrey. "My hart Sickens—and I feal as thou Some Secluded Spot Where abare Subsistance could be had Would be agreate releaf to My Soul."[13]

John Hogan, too, was appalled by the explosive atmosphere, even though he had contributed his share to creating the crisis. When he met Beecher and Gilman on the street one day, he appealed to Beecher for help. Couldn't he think of something that would allay the growing excitement, Hogan asked. Beecher thought he could. He still believed that if the prominent businessmen of the city would publicly announce their determination to maintain the law, all would be immediately peaceful. Already he had framed a set of resolutions that he believed would solve the problem. If his proposals were put into effect, he was convinced Lovejoy could soon resume publication of the *Observer*. Gilman suggested calling another public meeting to give Beecher an opportunity to try his plan. Although Hogan had little understanding of Beecher's ideas, he was desperate for any sort of accommodation and readily agreed to act as host for the meeting. He invited some of the prominent merchants and professional men, together with some of the clergy, to come to his store on Thursday, November 2, for an important conference. In his invitation he gave the impression that Beecher was ready to present a plan of compromise drafted by the abolitionists.[14]

. . . . .

[12] *Ibid.*, pp. 37-38; Tanner, *Martyrdom*, p. 136.

[13] Winthrop S. Gilman's account, November 9, 1837, Lovejoy Collection; Beecher, *Narrative*, p. 63; Godfrey to Theron Baldwin, November 4, 1837 (Library, Monticello College, Godfrey, Illinois).

[14] Beecher, *Narrative*, p. 52; Lovejoy, *Memoir*, p. 269.

Beecher dominated this meeting much as he had the gathering on October 30. Lovejoy was not present this time. He had stayed at home to guard his house, which had been attacked twice in recent days. Stones had been thrown through his windows, and on one occasion he had returned home to find his wife and son huddled in the attic, where they had taken refuge when men tried to break down the doors. Others would have to arrange the conditions of peace. Lovejoy's great need was to arrange conditions for his own survival.[15]

Hogan opened the proceedings by explaining why he had called the prominent men of Alton together. He hoped, he said, "to find some common ground on which both parties might meet . . . by mutual concession. . . . " Then he introduced Edward Beecher, who delivered a long speech in defense of civil rights, ending with the presentation of nine formal resolutions in support of free speech.

Aware of the critical importance of the meeting, Beecher used every sort of appeal he could think of in an effort to sway the neutral group assembled to hear him. He had come not to plead for individuals, he told his audience, but for principles "the importance of which language cannot utter." The men now listening to him were obliged not to remain neutral in the present crisis. It was their duty to defend actively those laws that were fundamental to the existence of civil society. If the mob triumphed in Alton, the authority of law throughout the state would be weakened. As property owners whose fortunes depended on law, they should maintain civil authority for their own material interests. He reminded them once more "that they were acting on the great theater of the world, and in the midst of attentive nations," and that they bore an obligation to their ancestors and to the future to preserve and transmit the liberties they had inherited.

The free communication of thoughts and opinions is one of the fundamental rights of man, Beecher declared, and the question of its abuse must be decided by the regular civil courts, not by a mob. When discussion is free and unrestrained, the triumph of the truth is certain, he told them, and with its triumph the return of peace is sure. He concluded by pleading specifically for the defense of Lovejoy and his press "on grounds of principle solely . . . to print and publish whatever he

. . . . .

[15] Beecher, *Narrative,* p. 90.

pleases, in obedience to the supreme laws of the land, and under the guidance and directions of the constituted civil authorities. . . ."[16]

When Beecher finished, he received only silence. Lovejoy's principal advocate had failed to break through the wall of prejudice in Alton. The address was probably Beecher's greatest performance, the most impressive in all his long and notable career, but his efforts had been totally wasted on that audience. No one offered to support his resolutions, no one suggested that his noble views pertained to Alton's crisis. It was a tragic moment for a man whose views were so elevated, whose faith in man's goodness and reasonableness was so strong, whose devotion to a cause he believed right was so unswerving.

While Beecher had been speaking, Usher F. Linder and others identified with extreme opposition to Lovejoy had entered Hogan's store. Thus reinforced, the voices of dissent would presently be heard. After a moment of embarrassed silence, someone moved to table Beecher's resolutions in defense of free speech. Other speakers then announced that they had been duped. They had come to Hogan's meeting supposing that Beecher was going to propose a compromise; instead, he had suggested total surrender to the abolitionists. The meeting was just another abolitionist trick. Linder declared that there was no reason to pass such resolutions anyway, for the Bill of Rights already contained similar ideas; and to pass them would be to condemn certain men now sitting in that very room who "had promoted, or at least connived at what had been done. . . ." Anyway, it was too much to expect, Linder added, that any party should admit itself entirely in the wrong.[17]

So much contention alarmed Hogan, who had called the meeting in the interest of peace. Attempting to soothe the objectors, he declared that he believed the spirit of Beecher's resolutions was good in general, and he hoped they might lead to a compromise that would produce unity and harmony.[18]

Such, of course, was the expectation that had brought men to the meeting. And for that reason the meeting was doomed to fail. Hogan

. . . . .

[16] *Ibid.*, pp. 53-59.
[17] *Ibid.*, p. 60.
[18] Lovejoy, *Memoir*, p. 270.

and others present had supposed that if each faction would begin by adopting a kindly and moderate view toward the other an agreement could then be arranged by rational processes. From the nature of the situation, however, any agreement would necessarily have been a compromise—an impossibility.

The abolitionists, unlike their opponents, could see no easy solution to the problem they faced. To them, moral principles seemed to be at stake that allowed no possible compromise. No exercise in logic or any other operation of the human mind could possibly have produced an agreement acceptable to them, for any compromise would disregard their conviction that problems of so great an import require difficult and stern moral decisions.

A moral decision in their minds involved duty, which they associated with religious obligation. No evasion of duty was possible. The human mind, unguided by reliance on divine illumination, appeared to them incompetent and human reason inadequate to arrange any substitute for the sober task of fulfilling a law that had already been made and (no matter how much the proud mind might rebel at the thought) was insusceptible to change by man.

Thus the abolitionists could not compromise, the mob refused to accept their principles, and the large neutral group declined to defend the rights of the abolitionists. The outcome of Hogan's meeting was therefore predictable. Another effort to create an atmosphere in which Lovejoy could resume his activities had failed.

Instead of passing Beecher's resolution, the meeting referred them to a committee composed of Hogan, Stephen Griggs, Usher F. Linder, H. G. Van Wagenen, Winthrop S. Gilman, Judge Thomas G. Hawley, and Cyrus Edwards, who was the state senator from Madison County, Whig candidate for governor, and brother of former governor Ninian W. Edwards. At the close of the meeting a resolution offered by Linder was passed which assured the antislavery group that if any violence were attempted before the meeting reassembled the next afternoon, those in attendance would aid in keeping order. The assembly thus gave evidence that it believed it had within itself the ability to maintain law and order within the city.[19]

That same evening, a few hours after Hogan's meeting had ad-

. . . . .

[19] *Ibid.*, pp. 270-271.

journed, the Alton Colonization Society convened again. John Hogan, Joel Parker, and John Mason Peck, a prominent Baptist preacher, all delivered speeches attacking abolitionist doctrine. With the assurance thus given that a prominent group in Alton remained staunch in support of colonization and unmoved by Beecher's appeals, the opponents of abolition could take a stronger stand than had seemed prudent at the meeting Thursday afternoon.[20]

The next morning Lovejoy and Beecher waited out the hours with their close friends until the meeting should reconvene and the committee's report be presented. This, they knew, would probably be their last chance to marshal the support of a majority in their defense, for the press was expected at any moment. If respectable men had not pledged themselves to maintain law by the time it arrived, violence would certainly occur with consequent destruction of property and perhaps even loss of life.

Beecher remained in his room at Lovejoy's house all morning, weighted down by the "momentous interests . . . at stake." Lovejoy and the Reverend Asa Hale visited him, and together they prayed. Lovejoy "interceded for the cause of God," Beecher wrote afterward, "and prayed especially for the best good of the community" of Alton. "He earnestly supplicated for an abiding sense of the presence of God and for strength that he might not betray his cause in the hour of trial."[21]

Beecher and Lovejoy thought they had some reason to hope for success. It seemed to them unlikely that a committee made up of educated and intelligent men could fail to recommend the adoption of Beecher's resolutions, which, after all, asked only for the maintenance of law. But no matter what the meeting might decide, Lovejoy had already settled on his course. He had abandoned his brief experiment of relying solely on moral suasion after the mob had assailed him at St. Charles. This press, he had decided, would be defended by armed force. A considerable number of citizens had agreed to help him protect it under guidance of civil authority, and the mayor had promised to fulfill his duties. The press, then, Lovejoy supposed, would be safe. The main consideration as he now saw it was his own personal safety, for he lived and worked in the midst of men who were his declared

. . . . .

[20] Beecher, *Narrative,* p. 64.

[21] *Ibid.,* p. 65.

enemies. Could he and his family avoid bodily harm? In spite of that persistent doubt, he had no intention of abandoning his responsibility as he had conceived it. Nearly isolated now from society and rejected by many of its leaders, he placed his entire reliance on God and faced the prospect of martydom willingly.[22]

Thus as Beecher and Lovejoy walked together through the streets of Alton toward Hogan's store early on Friday afternoon, they remained optimistic in spite of the formidable opposition arrayed against them. Beecher had not abandoned his faith in the goodness and reasonableness of mankind, and Lovejoy's position of resignation left him more nearly unconcerned with the outcome than would appear possible for most individuals so involved.

When the meeting reconvened at two o'clock, Linder was prepared to guide the afternon's business. Yesterday had belonged to Beecher. Today would be Linder's. He started the proceedings by offering the resolution that the meeting should "be composed exclusively of the citizens of Madison County." No one else should vote or take part in any discussion. Unanimously and without debate the resolution was passed. In that manner Linder excluded Beecher from participation in the meeting. Beecher was crushed by the action, for it involved far more than merely a personal affront. He now knew, even before the committee reported, that the meeting had rejected his appeal. They had ignored his grand concept that the situation in Alton involved principles vital to the whole nation and to future generations. How Lovejoy could henceforth be protected and the freedom of the press maintained was beyond anyone's knowledge. Certain that he had failed, Beecher "sat down in silent sadness to await the result."[23]

Cyrus Edwards then reported for the committee that had considered Beecher's resolutions. While the committee approved their "general spirit," Edwards said, it did not consider them "suited to the exigency" of the moment. They solely involved theories (that, of course, had been Beecher's plan in presenting them), but something more practical was needed, declared Edwards, for "parties are now organizing and arming for a conflict. . . . Under such circumstances, have we been convened." Quiet could be restored in Alton, he suggested, not by

. . . . .

[22] *Ibid.*, pp. 66-67.

[23] Lovejoy, *Memoir*, p. 271; Beecher, *Narrative*, p. 71.

the adoption of such abstract principles as Beecher had voiced, but by "nothing short of a generous forbearance, a mild spirit of conciliation, and a yielding compromise of conflicting claims." Beecher's resolutions, Edwards said—echoing Linder's words of the day before—demanded "too much of concession on one side, without equivalent concession on the other. . . . In this there is no compromise."

The committee, he said, wished to propose a set of substitute resolutions advising Lovejoy to "relinquish his interest and connection" with the *Observer*. "Such a course would highly contribute to the peace and harmony of the place and indicate on the part of the friends of the *Observer,* a disposition to do all in their power to restore the city to its accustomed harmony and quiet." Thus Lovejoy heard Alton's prominent citizens, after careful deliberation, reject his claims to a constitutional right to publish his newspaper.

Winthrop Gilman at once entered his protest to the committee report. "The rigid enforcement of law," he insisted, "would prove the only sure protection of the rights of citizens, and the only safe remedy for similar excitements in the future."

Linder spoke in favor of the Edwards resolutions, which he had helped to frame; but he added a sympathetic note: Lovejoy should be disgraced as little as possible, for he had a family dependent upon him. Everybody should feel sorry for Lovejoy, he added, "as an unfortunate man, whose hand was against every man and every man's hand against him."[24]

The meeting of neutrals from whom Beecher and Lovejoy had expected so much had turned completely against them. Now that a group of prominent men had formally requested Lovejoy to leave the city, it became his duty to present his own defense. He moved to the front of the room and calmly, without passion or display, began to speak to the men who had just announced their rejection of him.

> I feel, Mr. Chairman, that this is the most solemn moment of my life. I feel, I trust, in some measure the responsibilities which at this hour I sustain to these, my fellow citizens, to the church of which I am a minister, to my country, and to God. . . . Mr. Chairman, I do not admit that it is the business of this assembly to decide whether I shall or shall not publish a newspaper in this city. The gentlemen have, as the lawyers say, made a wrong issue. . . .
> . . . . .

[24] Lovejoy, *Memoir,* pp. 271-278.

I know that I have the right freely to speak and publish my sentiments, subject only to the laws of the land for the abuse of that right. . . . Mr. Chairman, what have I to compromise? If freely to forgive those who have so greatly injured me, if to pray for their temporal and eternal happiness, if still to wish for the prosperity of your city and state, notwithstanding all the indignities I have suffered in it; if this be the compromise intended, then do I willingly make it. . . .

But if by a compromise is meant that I should cease from doing that which duty requires of me, I cannot make it. And the reason is, that I fear God more than I fear man. . . . I know I am but one and you are many. My strength would avail but little against you all. You can crush me if you will; but I shall die at my post, for I cannot and will not forsake it. . . . Sir, the very act of retreating will embolden the mob to follow me wherever I go. No, sir; there is no way to escape the mob, but to abandon the path of duty: and that, God helping me, I will never do. . . .

And now you come together for the purpose of driving out a confessedly innocent man, for no cause but that he dares to think and speak as his conscience and his God dictate. . . . Pause, I beseech you, and reflect. The present excitement will soon be over; the voice of conscience will at last be heard. And in some season of honest thought, even in this world, as you review the scenes of this hour, you will be compelled to say, "He was right; he was right!"

. . . I am hunted as a partridge upon the mountains. I am pursued as a felon through your streets; and to the guardian power of the law I look in vain for that protection against violence, which even the vilest criminal may claim. . . .

Sir, I dare not flee away from Alton. . . . No, sir, the contest has commenced here; and here it must be finished. Before God and you all, I here pledge myself to continue it, if need be, till death. If I fall, my grave shall be made in Alton.[25]

Overcome with emotion, Lovejoy left the room as soon as he had finished speaking, and the meeting proceeded without him. His address had made a powerful impact on most of the audience and had turned sentiment momentarily in his favor. Unfortunately for the peace of the city, however, John Hogan obtained the floor as soon as Lovejoy had left. Yesterday Hogan had been in favor of compromise and moderation; today he was under Linder's influence. No matter what Lovejoy's abstract rights might be, Hogan insisted, he ought to abstain from exercising them in the present circumstances. He referred again to the pledge Lovejoy was thought to have given when he first arrived in Alton, and although Frederick Graves explained once more Love-

. . . . .

[25] Beecher, *Narrative,* pp. 85-91.

joy's exact remarks on that occasion, the harm had been done. Obviously the opposition was not going to yield. It remained unmoved by Beecher's appeal to reason and responsibility, unaffected by Lovejoy's eloquent appeal to sentiment.

Linder then took over. At the start of his long, rancorous, and abusive speech, he declared that he had just obtained a fresh insight into local affairs. Now he saw the situation more clearly than ever before. The issue, he said, was whether the citizens of Alton should themselves decide matters or whether they were to be dictated to by "foreigners" interested only in the "gratification of their own inclinations, and the establishment of certain abstract principles. . . . " He concluded by offering the resolution that the *Observer*'s policy had been and would continue to be destructive to peace, and that in no circumstance should it be re-established. The work of the mob, he suggested, ought to be regarded as having settled the matter.

Cyrus Edwards, recognizing the dangerous effect Linder's intemperate and provocative speech might have, urged the meeting to table Linder's resolution and proceed in a calmer manner. The assembly then took up the report Edwards had presented, accepting part of it. While they agreed both to entertain "a strong confidence" that citizens would "discountenance every act of violence" and "to cherish a sound regard for the bill of Rights," they also resolved that it was "a matter indispensable to the peace and harmony of this community that the labours and influence of the late Editor of the 'Observer' be no longer identified with any newspaper establishment in this city." Lovejoy had received the equivalent of an order to leave Alton.

As the meeting drew to an end, the crowd passed Linder's resolution against the *Observer,* another offered by Judge Hawley disapproving "all unlawful violence," and finally one offered by Mayor Krum to "regret that persons and editors from abroad have seen proper to interest themselves so conspicuously in the discussion and agitation of a question in which our city is made the principal theater." The discussion continued, finally centering upon Lovejoy's character and conduct. The moderating effects of his address had by that time been completely obliterated.[26]

. . . . .

[26] Lovejoy, *Memoir,* pp. 276-278; Tanner, *Alton Riots,* p. 8; Boston *Liberator,* December 22, 1837.

Two things were clear as the citizens adjourned: Lovejoy had repeated his determination never to abandon his work and never to leave Alton, and at the same time, those attending the meeting had made it equally clear that he would not be allowed to edit the *Observer* within the city. With the adjournment of Hogan's meeting, the last hope disappeared that reason could bring the leaders of Alton to protect Lovejoy and his press. Both Beecher and Lovejoy had failed with their program of moral suasion. The majority could not be won over and had utterly refused to accept the view that they bore a solemn responsibility to maintain civil rights. If the newspaper were to remain in Alton, it would have to be constantly defended by force. How Lovejoy himself was to be protected in that kind of hostile atmosphere, no one could say.

The Riots at Alton

Chapter XIII

Having made the crucial decision to defend the press by force, Lovejoy and Gilman now appealed to the civil authorities for support. They visited Mayor Krum and suggested that he authorize them to form a military company and either take command of it himself or deputize one of its members to act as his special agent in the event of disorder. The mayor readily admitted the need for such a company, because as he observed, no organized militia existed in Alton, and thus there was no constituted force he could depend on in an emergency. But he declined to command such a company himself. On the other hand, he said, private citizens were empowered to form one whenever they thought it necessary. Lovejoy insisted that they wanted to organize under the mayor's authority. The most that Mayor Krum would do, however, was to explain the state law on establishing militia companies and lend his law books to those interested.[1]

Soon afterward Gilman reported to Krum that the supporters of a free press had organized an informal company with William Harned as captain. The mayor seemed pleased and promised to use the force to maintain order if he found it necessary. He even agreed to appoint Harned as special deputy, although he withdrew this commission a little later when he found that he lacked the authority to appoint such officers.[2]

. . . . .

[1] Krum's testimony, Lincoln, *Alton Trials,* p. 38.

[2] *Ibid.,* pp. 38, 44.

Meanwhile, with the press due to arrive at any hour, the abolitionists made careful plans to protect it. Lovejoy believed the mob was most likely to attack while the press was being unloaded at the wharf. If, however, they could elude the public wrath at that moment and store the press in some defensible building, it would probably be safe. The press had been consigned to Amos Roff, who had offered to keep it in his hardware store until Lovejoy could arrange a site for a permanent office. But now objections appeared to this arrangement. Roff's store could not be easily defended, and the owner of the building refused to approve the storage of an article that might invite damage to his property.[3]

Winthrop Gilman agreed to keep the press temporarily in his large warehouse, a great stone structure on Water Street directly beside the Mississippi River. The press could be landed at his wharf, moved quickly across the street into the warehouse, and be safe there behind massive, nearly impregnable walls. In preparation for the arrival of the press, guns were moved from Roff's store to the warehouse. At the mayor's suggestion they were concealed in boxes so that no one on the streets would learn of the defense plans.[4]

One problem remained, however. The warehouse might provide an excellent storage place, but was there a wharf in Alton where the press could be landed without violence? Lovejoy's friends decided that the most prudent course would be to have the boat unload the press somewhere near the city; then they would convey it secretly to the warehouse. Late in October they made arrangements with an agent in St. Louis to notify the boat's captain to land at Chippewa, a point about five miles below Alton.[5]

All day on Friday, November 3, they kept a wagon and a team of horses waiting for the boat, but it failed to arrive. Since rain had fallen for many hours and the roads would soon be too muddy for travel, they decided to change their plans. The press would have to be landed at Alton after all.

They drove back to the city and sent a hurried message to St. Louis, advising their agent to instruct the captain to arrive at Gilman's

. . . . .

[3] *Ibid.*, p. 36.

[4] *Ibid.*; Gilman's account, November 9, 1837, Lovejoy Collection.

[5] S. E. Moore to Gilman, October 30, [1837], Lovejoy Collection.

wharf at three o'clock in the morning, the hour that seemed to them the least likely time for a mob to gather.

On Sunday, November 5, the long-expected news arrived from St. Louis. The *Missouri Fulton* had docked. It would reach Alton with the press on Tuesday morning at three o'clock.[6]

When Gilman received this news, he grew nervous at the prospect. By nature a cautious man, he could not forget that the warehouse and its contents were worth $30,000, half owned by Benjamin Godfrey, who by now had lost most of his sympathy for abolitionists and their problems. But in spite of the risk, the security of the press meant much to Gilman, and he determined to do all within his power to make certain the building would be defended. He called on the mayor once more and explained the situation. More than likely a mob would try to capture the press, he said. Did a citizen have the right to defend his property in such a circumstance? Mayor Krum assured him that he would be justified in repelling an attack and gave the impression that he personally would aid in defending the warehouse. Gilman urged him once again to appoint special constables to help protect the building. Krum repeated that he had no authority to do so. But, he added, the Common Council of Alton would meet later that day, and he would take the matter up with them.[7]

According to the minutes of the meeting, Krum told the Council "he had much reason to believe that the peace of the city would be disturbed: and he submitted to the Council the propriety of authorizing him to appoint special constables to aid in the maintenance of order." The Council, however, took no action. Instead, Councilman King moved "that the Mayor and Common Council address a note to Mr. Lovejoy and his friends, requesting them to relinquish the idea of establishing an abolition press at this time, in the city, and setting forth the expediency of the course." In this manner an important branch of the city government abdicated its responsibility to help maintain law and order.[8]

That same evening a group of ten or fifteen men assembled at the river to wait for the *Missouri Fulton*. Armed with clubs and pistols

. . . . .

[6] Gilman's account, November 9, 1837, Lovejoy Collection.

[7] Krum's testimony, Lincoln, *Alton Trials,* pp. 39-40.

[8] Lincoln, *Alton Trials,* p. 32.

and concealing themselves as best they could, they planned to seize the press before it could be taken to a storage place. But the boat did not arrive, and when the hour grew late, they decided to give up the watch and go home.[9]

While these men had been waiting at the wharf to wreck the press, another group of nearly forty men had met inside Godfrey and Gilman's warehouse to form a volunteer militia company under the laws of the state. Armed with loaded rifles and muskets, thirty of them waited out the hours until the *Missouri Fulton* should appear at the wharf across Water Street. Elijah Lovejoy was not present. He had remained at home, partly to care for his wife, who, expecting her second child and worn out from constant fear, was now confined to her bed most of the time, and partly to guard his own house, which intruders menaced almost nightly. In Lovejoy's absence, Gilman kept vigil at the warehouse.[10]

At three o'clock Tuesday morning Gilman saw the *Missouri Fulton* steaming up the river in the distance. He and Amos Roff hurried to Mayor Krum's house to warn him that the critical moment had arrived. The mayor agreed to go with them to the wharf while the press was unloaded and help maintain order in the event a crowd should gather. The three returned to the warehouse, where Harned, the leader of the militia company, offered the company's services to the mayor. Again Krum assured them that if the need arose he would welcome—indeed expect—their aid in suppressing any violence. Meanwhile, he said, they should guard the warehouse day and night, not leaving it unattended for a moment. Then, while the thirty men in the militia company remained inside the building, Gilman and Krum went down to the wharf while the boat's crew prepared to unload the large wooden box that held the press.[11]

At the hour scheduled for the boat to arrive, Lovejoy back at his house had awakened Edward Beecher, and together they walked toward the river. The city was quiet. "The moon had set," Beecher remembered, "and it was still dark, but day was near; and here and there a light was glimmering from the window of some sick room, or of some

. . . . .

[9] Edward Keating's testimony, *ibid.*, p. 13; Beecher, *Narrative*, p. 99.
[10] Beecher, *Narrative*, p. 100; Lovejoy, *Memoir*, p. 283.
[11] Krum's testimony, Lincoln, *Alton Trials*, pp. 39, 43.

early riser. The streets were empty and silent, and the sounds of our feet echoed from the walls as we passed along."[12]

When they came in sight of the river, the *Missouri Fulton* still lay at the wharf, and they saw with relief that no crowd had gathered. The press, Gilman assured them, rested safely inside the building. All had gone quietly. Someone had thought he heard a horn farther up the shore, and for a moment, in their nervousness, they had feared this was the signal for a mob to gather, but nothing at all had happened and the crew had carried the press safely inside the thick stone walls of Gilman's building.[13]

Feeling that a great victory had been won, Beecher and Lovejoy went into the warehouse and helped carry the box holding the press up to the third floor. There, they believed, it would surely be secure. Apparently, then, Beecher's efforts to still opposition had been more effective than he had supposed. With the greatest danger seemingly passed, the thirty men in the militia company agreed that their entire force was no longer needed at the warehouse. They would divide into sections of six, each to keep guard on successive nights during the next week. Since no mob would be likely to appear before morning, all the militiamen went home, and Beecher and Lovejoy remained alone inside the warehouse.[14]

"The morning soon began to dawn," Beecher later recalled, "and that morning I shall never forget. Who that has stood on the banks of the mighty stream that then rolled before me can forget the emotions of sublimity that filled his heart, as in imagination he has traced those channels of intercourse opened by it and its branches through the illimitable regions of this western world? I thought of future ages, and of the countless millions that should dwell on this mighty stream; and that nothing but the truth would make them free."[15]

As the dawn broke, the two men climbed through the scuttle to the roof and ascended to the highest point of the wall. "The sky and the river were beginning to glow with approaching day," Beecher remembered, "and the busy hum of business [could] be heard." As they

. . . . .

[12] Beecher, *Narrative,* p. 100.
[13] Lovejoy, *Memoir,* p. 283.
[14] Beecher, *Narrative,* p. 101.
[15] *Ibid.*

looked exultingly at the scene below, Beecher believed that "a bloodless battle had been gained for God and for the truth; and that Alton was redeemed from eternal shame." Lovejoy appeared "tranquil and composed . . . for he trusted in God that the point was gained: that the banner of an unfettered press would soon wave over that mighty stream."[16]

Thus confident in the press's safety, they returned to Lovejoy's house. Beecher decided to leave at once for Jacksonville, certain that he had been instrumental in winning a great victory for civil rights. The two men entered the sickroom where Celia Lovejoy lay. Together they prayed, and Beecher commended his hosts to the care of God. As he left the house to meet the stagecoach, he cheered Mrs. Lovejoy "with the hope that her days of trial were nearly over and that more tranquil hours were at hand."[17]

But later in the day, after Beecher had started on his trip, disquieting rumors spread through the city. By then it was generally known that the press had arrived and was stored in Gilman's warehouse. In the coffeehouses, as the saloons of Alton were called, one could hear ominous snatches of conversation that afternoon. Those men who hated the doctrine of abolition were making new plans.

Beecher was quite mistaken in supposing he had allayed hostility. Having failed to destroy the press at the wharf, the mob now resolved to take it by force. Both Gilman and Lovejoy heard the rumors and realized that their optimism of the early morning had been unwarranted. They now expected violence. Gilman sent his wife out of town, and Celia Lovejoy went to stay with a friend in Upper Alton.[18]

Toward evening, volunteers for Gilman's militia company began arriving at the warehouse. Lovejoy and a few local abolitionists were there, of course, but most of those who came were younger men intrigued with the idea of acting together to enforce the law. Few of them had any particular interest in abolition as such or even in protecting the press. Some were there simply to have a good time. As one explained later, "they expected to have some crackers and cheese and hear some good stories."[19] But, for whatever reason, forty-two men

. . . . .

[16] *Ibid.*, pp. 101-102.

[17] *Ibid.*, pp. 102-103.

[18] "Winthrop S. Gilman to Dr. Chandler Robbins Gilman, November 8, 1837," *Mississippi Valley Historical Review*, IV (1917-18), 493.

[19] Joseph Greeley's testimony, Lincoln, *Alton Trials*, p. 23.

appeared to sign the roll which formally organized a militia company under state law. After electing W. G. Attwood as captain, they climbed to the second story, took up loaded arms, and paraded and drilled for a while. At eight o'clock Attwood asked for volunteers who would stay and defend the building that night. Fourteen men stepped forward. The rest left.[20]

While Lovejoy stayed with the militia, Gilman and William L. Chappell went again to consult with the mayor. Did the militia have a legal right to defend the warehouse, Gilman wanted to know. Did it have the right to stay inside the building? The mayor assured Gilman, as he had done in the past, that the militia was perfectly legal and that he himself would command it to suppress a riot should he judge the situation required it.[21]

Meanwhile in the coffeehouses on Second Street as the night fell, men laid their plans to destroy the press. In the Tontine, Alton's most popular saloon, William Carr carried whiskey to the men ranged around the walls and enlisted their aid. Warmed with drink, men became outspoken that night. David Butler, who had been cursing abolitionists in general, was heard to declare in a loud voice that he "would have the press." Small groups gathered in the streets outside the coffeehouses to await further developments. About ten o'clock the first part of the mob left the Tontine, formed itself into a column, and marched toward the warehouse.[22]

John Solomon, a young man whom Gilman had once befriended, had heard what was about to happen. Wanting to do Gilman a good turn, he reported the plan to Edward Keating. Keating summoned Henry H. West, Linder's brother-in-law, and together they hurried to inform Gilman what the mob intended to do. Plans had been made either to burn the warehouse or to blow it up, they reported. Gilman was much shocked at the news. He had expected a disturbance, but he had not supposed the situation to be so desperate. He asked the men to bring the mayor at once.[23]

Keating hurried to the mayor's office and gave him the alarming report. Krum did not go to the warehouse immediately, however. In-

. . . . .

[20] *Ibid.*, p. 22.

[21] Krum's testimony, *ibid.*, pp. 40-41.

[22] Greeley's testimony, *ibid.*, p. 112; Samuel Miller's testimony, *ibid.*, p. 110; Webb C. Quigley's testimony, *ibid.*, pp. 115-116.

[23] Henry H. West's testimony, *ibid.*, p. 15; Keating's testimony, *ibid.*, pp. 10-12.

stead, he walked down the street a few doors to the office of Dr. Hart, who was known to be a determined opponent of abolitionist doctrine. While they conferred, the first detachment of the mob marched by. One of the men, the mayor saw, carried a gun. He then sent for Judge Martin and other civil officers. When they did not arrive at once, he and Sherman Robbins, a justice of the peace, started off toward the warehouse.[24]

By that time the mob had arrived in front of the stout structure. If they expected to storm the warehouse easily, they would be disappointed. One gabled end of the warehouse fronted the river; the other faced Water Street. Only the gabled ends had windows and doors; the other sides were solid masonry. Although vacant lots bounded the warehouse on two sides, leaving the building open to attack from all directions, it nonetheless appeared to be easily defensible.[25]

On their way from the Tontine, the mob had picked up stones from the streets. As soon as they reached the building, they began pelting the windows and doors. Lovejoy and the other defenders inside the building waited, uncertain of the best action to take. Gilman decided to make a personal appeal. He opened an upper door and began to address the crowd. It was a clear moonlight night, and they could see him distinctly. As he appeared above them, they fell back in a line with their backs to the river, somewhat abashed at being confronted by Alton's richest and most prominent citizen.

He was sorry, he said, that they had come at such an unusual hour to create a disturbance. What did they want?

"The press," answered William Carr, spokesman for the mob.

Gilman replied that, while he bore no ill feelings toward anyone and would regret to injure any person, he felt it his duty to protect his property and would do so at the risk of his life.

Carr shouted the reply. They had not come to hurt him or to damage his property. But they were determined to destroy the press at the sacrifice of *their* lives. With that, someone flourished a pistol toward Gilman, who hastily withdrew from the opening and shut the door.[26]

. . . . .

[24] Krum's testimony, *ibid.*, p. 41.

[25] Tanner, *Alton Riots*, p. 10.

[26] Miller's testimony, Lincoln, *Alton Trials*, p. 110; Gilman's account, November 9, 1837, Lovejoy Collection.

The men below began throwing stones again, breaking most of the windows in the end of the building toward the river. From inside the warehouse, a shower of crockery answered the mob's barrage. It would be only one step from the use of stones to the use of guns. Henry H. West sensing the temper of the mob, returned to the warehouse to urge Gilman not to let the defenders use their weapons. His efforts were in vain. Someone from the outside fired. An answering shot precipitated a general volley. West then pleaded with the defenders to direct their fire over the heads of the crowd. Lovejoy replied that not a shot must be wasted. While buckshot filled the air, the captain of the steamboat *Ark,* sailing up the river in front of the warehouse, veered his craft toward the far shore in order to avoid the fire.[27]

Suddenly a shout went up outside the warehouse. Someone in the crowd had been hit. Lyman Bishop, a young carpenter recently arrived from western New York, was being carried away, mortally wounded. The shock caused the mob to fall back temporarily, and for a few minutes all was quiet. At that moment the mayor finally arrived in front of the warehouse to confront the mob and the crowd of spectators, who by that time filled the streets. Although the night was cold, Solomon Morgan ran to join the crowd, barefoot and in his shirt sleeves. The mayor tried to stop him, but Morgan tore himself away, shouting the ever-present question, "How would you like a damned nigger going home with your daughter?" Dr. Beall, moving through the crowd, was heard to say that he would like "to kill every damned abolitionist in town." When Justice Robbins ordered Levi Palmer to go home, Palmer grabbed him by the shoulders and told him that *he* had better go home, for they intended to take the press.[28]

The mob was clearly in no mood to respond to authority. When the mayor, standing on a box, finally got their attention, they refused to leave at his command. Though several peace officers had arrived by that time, no force outside the warehouse was sufficient to dispel the mob. Their spokesmen convinced the mayor that they would not

. . . . .

[27] Tanner, *Alton Riots,* p. 11; West's testimony, Lincoln, *Alton Trials,* pp. 16-18; Peoria *Register,* November 11, 1837. None of the witnesses claimed that the first shot was fired from inside the warehouse, although some were uncertain as to where it originated. See Lincoln, *Alton Trials,* pp. 10, 97, 103.

[28] Webb Quigley's testimony, Lincoln, *Alton Trials,* p. 115; Samuel Avis' testimony, *ibid.,* p. 113; Robbins' testimony, *ibid.,* p. 108.

leave until Lovejoy and Gilman had surrendered the press. Finally, Mayor Krum agreed to act as emissary for the mob and carry a message to the men inside—unless Lovejoy surrendered the press, the building would be burned. The mob promised to wait quietly until the mayor had returned with an answer.[29]

The mayor, accompanied by Robbins, delivered the ultimatum to Lovejoy and Gilman. Gilman begged the mayor to use his influence with important citizens to see if they could not find some way to disperse the mob and thus save both the press and the warehouse. It would be useless to try, the mayor answered. "So numerous and desperate was the mob," he explained later, "that it was impracticable to organize the citizens against them at that late hour and in that moment of excitement." But though he considered himself helpless to halt the violence, he once more assured Gilman that he possessed the legal right to defend his property and that the militia company had been completely justified in firing at their assailants.[30]

Gilman, Lovejoy, and the other defenders of the press were adamant in their refusal to surrender. Krum dreaded to relay that inciting news to the mob. He remained inside the warehouse longer than necessary, hoping that the delay would calm the crowd. But the effect of Bishop's death had been too great for that. The mob demanded vengeance. While the mayor was inside the building, they had carried an extension ladder from a nearby barn and raised it against the northwest corner of the warehouse, where shots fired from the inside could not reach. In the street men were starting a fire with which they would kindle the roof.[31]

The mayor finally summoned his courage and emerged from the warehouse to deliver Lovejoy's and Gilman's refusal to surrender the press. When the mob heard the news, a great shout went up. The mayor declared that the militia would fire if they did not disperse, but no one paid any attention to this threat. They hastened preparations to set fire to the roof.[32]

The church bells of the city now tolled over the frantic scene. Mrs.

. . . . .

[29] Krum's testimony, *ibid.*, p. 40.

[30] Gilman's account, November 9, 1837, Lovejoy Collection.

[31] Krum's testimony, Lincoln, *Alton Trials*, p. 42.

[32] *Ibid.*, p. 46; Lovejoy, *Memoir*, p. 290.

Frederick Graves, a semi-invalid, had gone into the Presbyterian church and started to ring the bells in the hope that help would come. The alarm served to summon more people to the warehouse area, until a crowd of at least 200 had gathered. No one, however, took any effective steps to end the violence. Judge William Martin urged the property owners among the spectators to help him restore order, but no one appeared willing to raise a hand against the mob.[33]

The assailants continued their plans for destruction, unaffected by either authority or public opinion. A man carrying a flaming torch climbed the ladder to set fire to the warehouse roof. Five of the defenders dashed out of the building and fired at him and then fired into the mob. For a moment the crowd fell back. Then they regained courage, and while men covered him from behind a pile of lumber, the incendiary climbed the ladder again, this time successfully igniting the wood-shingled roof. With the building afire and surrounded by an angry mob, the position of the defenders became desperate.[34]

Royal Weller and Elijah Lovejoy came out of the warehouse and aimed their pistols at the figure on the ladder. Almost as soon as they appeared at the door, the men behind the lumber pile fired, striking both Lovejoy and Weller. Weller was injured only slightly. Lovejoy, hit by five bullets, fell back into the building, struggled up the first flight of stairs, and there in the counting room on the second story fell lifeless to the floor.[35]

The roof of the warehouse was blazing now, and the mob had the situation under their control. With Lovejoy dead and the building afire, the defenders could see no purpose in continuing the struggle and no alternative but to surrender. In the hope of arranging terms with the mob, Amos Roff stepped outside. Immediately he was shot and wounded. West then pounded on the door again. "For God's sake leave the building and let them in," he cried, "or all the property will be destroyed."[36]

With West's aid, all the defenders but the wounded and Thaddeus

. . . . .

[33] Tanner, *Martyrdom,* p. 225; Krum's testimony, Lincoln, *Alton Trials,* p. 102; Martin's testimony, *ibid.,* p. 119.

[34] Gilman's account, November 9, 1837, Lovejoy Collection.

[35] *Ibid.*

[36] *Ibid.*

B. Hurlbut, who stayed behind with Lovejoy, fled toward the river while the mob harassed them with buckshot. The warehouse stood open and defenseless, while Solomon Morgan encouraged the mob to "go and finish your work." Several men then entered the building, hoisted the press up to a window on the third floor, and dropped it to the street below. They disturbed nothing else in the warehouse. Dr. Beall saw to that. This was not to be an act of social upheaval. He warned those who entered the building that "he did not want the property injured, nor anything taken away."[37]

While West scrambled up the ladder to put out the fire with water that Dr. Hope carried from the river in West's hat, other men dragged the press to the steamboat landing and began smashing it with hammers. The behavior of those who broke up the press "was orderly—it was done in a quiet sort of way," a witness reported. "They seemed to be happy while engaged in breaking it in pieces."[38]

By midnight the affair was finished. Soon the bright moon that had lighted the scene went down; the bells and the guns and the hammers were silent, the clamorous streets empty. Peace came over the city as the people went home. Some remained behind to guard Lovejoy's body, and a few curious members of the mob climbed to the second floor of the warehouse to stare at their victim. The long struggle to defend the freedom of the press appeared to have ended in utter catastrophe.[39]

. . . . .

[37] West's testimony, Lincoln, *Alton Trials,* p. 97; Samuel Miller's testimony, *ibid.,* p. 111.

[38] Greeley's testimony, *ibid.,* p. 23; West's testimony, *ibid.,* pp. 95-96.

[39] "Winthrop S. Gilman to Dr. Chandler Robbins Gilman, November 8, 1837," *Mississippi Valley Historical Review,* IV (1917-18), 493.

Aftermath

Chapter XIV

Elijah Lovejoy now lay dead on the second floor of Winthrop Gilman's warehouse, while in the street below a mob destroyed the symbol of his influence and cast its fragments into the river waters. Thus had disaster overtaken a man who only ten years earlier had walked toward the West in the assurance that he could promote the renovation of an erring world.

In some earlier, more settled time such a man as Lovejoy might willingly have remained at home in New England and as a Puritan among Puritans exercised the influence of a respected leader. But that time had passed, for change was upsetting the old New England order. Lovejoy came out of a section and out of a class that clearly saw power and authority slipping from its control during the first quarter of the nineteenth century. New forces threatened to take from New England and the New England clergy their former dominance—political, economic, and cultural. The rising West with its ebullient democracy, the new industrialism with its moneyed society that little heeded the clergy's teachings, the emergent cotton kingdom completely beyond the control of Puritan New England—all these appeared as threats to the religious leaders of the Northeast.

With the decline of the established church and the emergence of ideals foreign to the Puritan mind and heart, men like Lovejoy became strangers in a world that was passing them by. In the face of such upheaval they could not remain quiescent. Action on their part seemed imperative. The reform program they initiated in this situation embraced the temporal aims of extending New England cultural influence into the new West and restoring to the clergy the control they had once exercised over Northern society. By striking at infidelity and Catholicism, at moral laxity and slavery, they aimed to assert their dominance over those areas of American life where the teachings of New England Protestantism were the most flagrantly ignored.[1]

But it would surely be a mistake to suppose that their comprehensive reform efforts were motivated solely by an uncomplicated human desire to reinforce their own declining status: there was evil in the world, and as religious men they felt a responsibility to do something about it. Personal ambition they no doubt had, along with many other human frailties, but such motives alone cannot explain their activity. Like all other men, the reformers were products of the past and not merely of their own time. The sense of mission experienced by the first Puritan settlers in New England had persisted in their descendants. God demanded much from His chosen people—in 1830 as in 1630. Many New Englanders, still bound by the covenant theology, kept that knowledge green. If sometimes they had seemed to flag in religious enterprise, periodically—as in Lovejoy's day—they reaffirmed their obligation to conform perfectly to God's law and to enlarge His kingdom. The successes of the British evangelical reform example had probably helped stimulate them to action; secular sources, too, had recently reinforced their inherited duty not to suffer sin and error. The Revolutionary generation, with its affirmation of the self-evident truths "that all men are created equal; that they are endowed by their Creator with certain unalienable rights," had bequeathed to the American reformers a secular task, which they were inclined to interpret in religious terms: America, they believed, had become God's special repository; He intended His will to be done here—in the loosening of bonds, in

. . . . .

[1] Evarts B. Greene, "A Puritan Counter-Reformation," American Antiquarian Society, *Proceedings,* n.s. XLII (1932), 17-46; Richard L. Power, "A Crusade to Extend Yankee Culture, 1820-1865," *New England Quarterly,* XIII (1940), 638-653. See also David Donald's suggestive essay, "Toward a Reconsideration of Abolitionists," in his *Lincoln Reconsidered* (New York, 1956), pp. 19-36. The view that the reformers were not genuinely opposed to the evils they crusaded against receives its strongest expression in Clifford S. Griffin, *Their Brothers' Keepers; Moral Stewardship in the United States, 1800-1865* (New Brunswick, New Jersey, 1960).

the removal of artificial distinctions, in the proclamation of liberty to all men. It thus became the Christian's responsibility to aid Him in the holy enterprise of sweeping away every man-made obstacle to pure religion, to virtue, and to freedom.

The reformers became in this way the heirs of Puritanism and the Enlightenment, pledged to help the nation achieve the goals of both traditions. Looking about them, they could see, even in their own neighborhoods, manifold sins and evils that measured the extent to which the nation had fallen short of achieving its expectations. For quite unselfish reasons the reformers became convinced of their duty to promote the salvation of sinners and to destroy those habits and institutions which contravened God's law and prevented man from enjoying his unalienable rights. Their success would enlarge God's kingdom, and it would bring American secular practice into accord with America's professed principles. If as a result of their benevolent efforts the reformers also should expand their own personal influence, who (they might have asked) could say that God's will, in even that detail, had not been done?

As a pious young man, Lovejoy had been drawn to the West by some such purpose. There, through the agency first of a classical high school, then of a political newspaper, and finally of an antislavery press, he attempted to throw the weight of his influence against the new powers rising in America. Like many another man of similar background, he eventually focused his entire opposition against slavery—the nation's most conspicuous evil, the sum of everything the clergy most deplored, the objective correlative of the new forces overshadowing them. But by so doing, he encountered a foe too powerful to beat down, and in his death the New England clergy suffered another in a long series of defeats at the hand of a society that was in the process of rejecting their ideals.[2]

It was Lovejoy's misfortune to settle in a spot where the contest between the new and the old ideals was exceptionally keen. He promulgated his views first in a slave state and then in a Northern border city, whose social and economic ties with the South were intimate, whose government was weak. Local politicians in Alton used the widespread

. . . . .

[2] Merton L. Dillon, "The Failure of the American Abolitionists," *Journal of Southern History,* XXV (May, 1959), pp. 159-177.

prejudice against Negroes to serve their own political fortunes and, as a result, opposed Lovejoy in order to further their own careers. Lovejoy embodied the Puritan religious spirit in its most tenacious form. His peculiar idea of responsibility prohibited him from modifying his stand, whatever the consequence to himself or the community. Encountering inevitable opposition, he proclaimed his rights only the more ardently, rights that according to American tradition were undoubtedly his. But his opponents refused to respect those rights, asking in effect whether society is bound to give a hearing to doctrines, however moral, that it believes dangerous; whether a democratic government, whose ultimate support rests on the people, must protect the advocate of doctrines the people deem wrong.[3]

In waging his reform campaigns, Lovejoy was neither wise nor prudent in the sense ordinarily accorded those words. Such attributes belonged instead to his opponents—not to the mob, of course, but to those moderates who sought to quell the discord in St. Louis and Alton by persuading him to be silent. Probably most of them shared Lovejoy's dislike for slavery in the abstract, but unlike him, they were willing to live with it in practice, whatever its enormities. They recognized that agitation against so pervasive an institution must upset many social arrangements, perhaps even destroying the Union and leading to war. In their judgment the maintenance of peace and the perpetuation of the existing social structure were more important than the destruction of human slavery. Therefore (following their reasoning) to refuse to agitate, but rather to wait, as they did, in the expectation that God in His own good time and by acts of His own providence would eventually end slavery was wise. Such an attitude no doubt revealed a healthy adjustment to society and its evils. But it was an attitude Lovejoy could not share. The probable consequences of agitation caused him no alarm. He believed the sin of slavery too horrendous to permit temporizing. He refused to wait; he attempted instead to direct events at ever accelerating speed toward the immediate abolition of slavery and the integration of the Negro into American life. Lovejoy, like other abolitionists, thereby marked himself as a revolutionary out of step with his times, as revolutionaries always

. . . . .

[3] Thomas Ford, *A History of Illinois,* p. 251.

are. It is useless to look for moderation and prudence in such men or to criticize them for lacking such qualities.

Although Lovejoy made an important—even a necessary—contribution to the antislavery movement, he still cannot be ranked with the very greatest of the abolitionists. As a human being he was of uncommon interest: men who struggle against tremendous obstacles for the sake of high principle perpetually engage our concern and our compassion; and if, in the course of those unequal contests, they themselves are destroyed, then their lives partake of tragedy, the noblest of dramatic forms. Lovejoy's role in the antislavery movement thus became that of the tragic hero. His personal destruction came to be thought of as a forecast of the fate all human liberty must suffer if slavery should be perpetuated. For that reason he was more influential among abolitionists because of his failure than because of his success. Certainly his significance did not lie in his contribution to antislavery thought. Although he was an able reform writer and editor, few of his ideas can be called original. He developed no new arguments or techniques for advancing the abolitionist crusade as did Garrison and Birney; neither was he a great organizer of antislavery forces as was Weld. His importance stems rather from the fact that he was killed by a mob while defending the abstract principles of civil liberty, particularly the freedom of the press.

Because Lovejoy stood firmly for those principles, he died; and with his death freedom of the press lost a great battle. Although the civil rights tradition was too strong in the United States for that freedom to be snuffed out, it was maintained in spite of, rather than because of, the riots at Alton. In the long run, it is true, Lovejoy became a symbol of the fight for a free press—but because he lost, not because he won. Only out of the revulsion produced by his death did a conscience-stricken North, moving ever closer to war against the institution Lovejoy had condemned, decide that he had been right.

His death brought no immediate victory in Alton. If throughout most of the North there was horror at his murder, there was little contrition in Alton itself. A month after the riot Gideon Blackburn reported from Carlinville that the mob at Alton still ruled. Owen Lovejoy made a similar observation, and even four years afterward an abolitionist visiting the city felt compelled to report that "*Lower* Alton still glories in blood." Men could be found in later years who would even boast that they had fired the shot that killed Lovejoy. Nor did freedom of the press immediately become secure in Illinois. The editor of the Peoria *Register* was compelled to resign in 1843 because he refused to stop printing antislavery articles.[4]

Neither were those responsible for the riots punished. In January, 1838, some alleged members of the mob were brought to trial at Alton. But strangely enough, their trial was preceded by the prosecution of Winthrop S. Gilman and other defenders of the press for the crime of riot on the ground that by organizing to use force they had unlawfully defended Gilman's warehouse. Usher F. Linder dominated both trials. After Gilman's trial had started, Judge William Martin received a petition requesting that Linder be permitted to aid the city attorney in conducting the prosecution. Judge Martin admitted him to the proceedings. In the second trial, Linder defended the members of the mob. The jury returned a verdict of "not guilty" for all parties in both trials; thus no one was ever convicted for either the destruction of the press or the murder of Lovejoy. Nothing whatsoever seemed to have been gained in Alton.[5]

Lovejoy's murder did bring accessions to the Northern antislavery societies, however, and persuaded men to join them who would perhaps not have done so had they not seen civil liberties endangered. Knowledge that this probably would happen helped Lovejoy's associates interpret his death as more than a meaningless sacrifice. Edward Beecher, for a time completely overwhelmed by the news of the events in Alton, at last found consolation for the death of his friend in the conviction that "his enemies have failed in their purpose & he has triumphed in his fall." Owen Lovejoy, too, was confident that his brother had accomplished more by dying than "living and unopposed he could have done in a century." "Thousands of our citizens, who lately believed that they had nothing to do with the subject of slavery, now begin to discover their error," commented the officials of the

. . . . .

[4] Blackburn to Absalom Peters, December 6, 1837, AHMS Papers; Lowell (Illinois) *Genius of Liberty,* January 30, 1841; Samuel E. Chamberlain, *My Confession* (New York, 1956), p. 31; Chicago *Western Citizen,* February 23, 1843; Ernest E. East, "Samuel H. Davis," Mt. Sterling (Illinois) *Democrat-Message,* July 28, 1948.

[5] Lincoln, *Alton Trials, passim.*

Illinois Anti-Slavery Society at their anniversary meeting in 1838.[6]

Throughout the North, the death of Lovejoy created enormous resentment. The Alton riots supplied persuasive evidence to illustrate the "bloodthirstiness" of the "slave power." Sermons on the subject were preached from practically every pulpit, and protest meetings were held in almost every village. Probably no other event produced so great an impact on Northern opinion before the execution of John Brown in 1859.[7]

The American Anti-Slavery Society, officially adopting Lovejoy as a martyr, issued writing paper bearing a crest with the legend, "LOVEJOY the first MARTYR to American LIBERTY. MURDERED for asserting the FREEDOM of the PRESS. Alton Nov. 7, 1837." But Lovejoy did not receive the title of martyr without opposition from the nonresistance wing of the antislavery movement. Back in the East, Benjamin Lundy criticized Lovejoy's physical defense of his press, and Sarah Grimké mourned that abolitionists had resorted to "physical force, to the weapons of death to defend the cause of God. . . . " Theirs, however, was a minority voice. Most abolitionists decided to capitalize on the event to further their cause, and this they did effectively.[8]

Holding an emergency session of its executive committee, the American Anti-Slavery Society arranged to take advantage of the general revulsion of feeling that followed the murder. It made plans to hold a well-publicized commemorative service in the Broadway Tabernacle in New York City, complete with a funeral dirge and a sermon preached by the abolitionist Beriah Green. It also authorized the printing of an extra 40,000 copies of the issue of its publication *Human Rights,* which detailed the events in Alton. Abolitionist leaders hoped to bring Lovejoy's body from Illinois to New England for burial, and Joseph C. Lovejoy, his brother, speculated with pleasure on the pros-

. . . . .

[6] Beecher to Owen Lovejoy, November 14, 1837, Owen Lovejoy Papers; Owen Lovejoy to Henry George Chapman, December 9, 1837, Chapman Papers, Anti-Slavery Collection (Boston Public Library); Minutes of the Illinois Anti-Slavery Society, pp. 65-66 (Chicago Historical Society).

[7] Joseph Lovejoy to Owen Lovejoy, December 7, 1837, Owen Lovejoy Papers; for the national reaction, see Hazel C. Wolf, *On Freedom's Altar, the Martyr Complex in the Abolition Movement* (Madison, Wisconsin, 1952), pp. 45-48.

[8] S. W. Benedict to Owen Lovejoy, July 2, 1838, Owen Lovejoy Papers; Philadelphia *National Enquirer,* November 16 and 23, 1837; Sarah Grimké to Sarah Douglass, November 23, 1837, Barnes and Dumond (eds.), *Weld-Grimké Letters,* I, 480-481.

pect of a funeral reaching over a distance of 1,800 miles. That plan was abandoned. Instead, Owen Lovejoy arranged to send his brother's widow from Illinois to visit the Lovejoy family in Maine. "Celia will be a great lion in the places through which she passes," he predicted. "If she is partly unwell I doubt not the impression she makes will be good." Lovejoy was scarcely dead before the executive committee commissioned his brothers to prepare a memoir, which was soon published with a foreword by John Quincy Adams, who was himself winning abolitionist praise as the defender of the right of petition against proslavery assaults. Edward Beecher made plans to prepare an account of the riots in which he would argue "not merely the question of right, but of the prudence and wisdom of the steps taken. . . ."[9]

These manifold activities produced the desired effect. Certainly many new members flocked into the antislavery societies when they realized for the first time that their own civil liberties might be imperiled as a result of the slavery controversy. But perhaps as important as these accessions was the shock the riots gave to the abolitionists.

"I can never forget the quick, sharp agony of that hour which brought us news of Lovejoy's death. . . . The gun fired at Lovejoy was like that of Sumter—it scattered a world of dreams," wrote the Boston abolitionist, Wendell Phillips, many years afterward.[10] The "world of dreams" scattered by the mob at Gilman's warehouse on that cold, moonlit night in 1837 was the bundle of illusions that had thus far surrounded the antislavery movement.

The antislavery movement had been founded on the idea of the essential goodness of all men (even of slaveholders), of their reasonableness, and of their capacity to be swayed by moral arguments addressed to their higher natures. The abolitionists' method had been that of religious revivalists. They had believed that if slaveowners were once informed of the sin of slavery, they would make haste to repent and out of contrition free their slaves. Although abolitionists discovered

. . . . .

[9] American Anti-Slavery Society, Minutes of the Executive Committee (Boston Public Library); Joseph Lovejoy to Owen Lovejoy, December 7, 1837, Owen Lovejoy Papers; Owen Lovejoy to Joseph Lovejoy, April 16, 1838, Wickett-Wiswall Collection; Joseph Lovejoy to Gerrit Smith, November 29, 1837, Lovejoy Collection; John Quincy Adams to Lewis Tappan, February 26, 1838, Adams Papers (Massachusetts Historical Society, Boston); Joseph Lovejoy to Owen Lovejoy, November 25, 1837, Lovejoy Collection.

[10] *Anti-Slavery Standard,* April 27, 1867, quoted in Melvin Jameson, *Elijah Parish Lovejoy as a Christian* (Rochester, New York, 1909), p. 113.

early in the 1830's that the South had sealed itself against antislavery ideas at the expense of civil rights, few had yet given up hope that moral suasion could still in some way end slavery in the United States. The stubborn resistance of the South to abolitionist argument, however, accompanied by equally stubborn opposition in the North, helped to shift the ideas of the Northern reformers. The murder of Lovejoy administered the final shock. To an increasing extent, abolitionists abandoned reliance on moral suasion. They would themselves defy the law to aid fugitive slaves; shortly they would enter politics; ultimately they would acquiesce in the use of military force. This fateful shift in method resulted largely from the realization that moral suasion simply did not work, either in the North or in the South. Beecher had proved that fact on repeated occasions in Alton; Lovejoy proved it when he was felled by an assassin's bullet.

When the abolitionists changed their methods, their optimism changed too. Material interest, they now concluded, exercised greater influence over the minds of men than religious argument and appeals for conformity to moral law. It appeared that Southerners, finding slave labor profitable and convenient and fearing the social results of giving freedom to Negroes, would never voluntarily end slavery. Nor did it seem much more likely that Northerners would with any degree of unanimity accept the abolitionist doctrine of racial equality. If the slaves were ever to be freed, direct action must supplant moral suasion. Slavery was not to be ended through religious revival. Lovejoy's death did more than anything else before the prolonged tensions of the 1850's to dissipate the optimism of the 1830's and to persuade Northerners of the hopelessness of the antislavery movement as a moral reform.

Zebina Eastman, an Illinois abolitionist, was correct when he wrote many years later that the new phase of antislavery agitation culminated in the redemption of the Negro in America from slavery.[11] But he expressed a truth perhaps more significant for an understanding of the history of the antislavery movement when he added that emancipation came not by moral reform but through the use of war power—in judgment unpreceded by repentance.

. . . . .

[11] Zebina Eastman, "History of the Anti-Slavery Agitation and the Growth of the Liberty and Republican Parties in the State of Illinois," Rufus Blanchard (ed.), *Discovery and Conquests of the North-West, with the History of Chicago* (Wheaton, Illinois, 1881), p. 663.

Bibliography

On the intellectual background of early nineteenth-century reformers, I have found the following particularly useful: Whitney R. Cross, *The Burned-over District: The Social and Intellectual History of Enthusiastic Religion in Western New York, 1800-1850* (Ithaca, New York, 1950); Charles Roy Keller, *The Second Great Awakening in Connecticut* (New Haven, Connecticut, 1942); Evarts Boutell Greene, "A Puritan Counter-Reformation," American Antiquarian Society, *Proceedings,* n.s. XLII (1932), 17-46; Richard Lyle Power, "A Crusade to Extend Yankee Culture, 1820-1865," *New England Quarterly,* XIII (1940), 638-653; John R. Bodo, *The Protestant Clergy and Public Issues, 1812-1848* (Princeton, New Jersey, 1954); and Charles C. Cole, Jr., *The Social Ideas of the Northern Evangelists, 1826-1860* (New York, 1954).

The relation between American and English evangelical religion and the reform movements is discussed in Charles I. Foster, *An Errand of Mercy; the Evangelical United Front, 1790-1837* (Chapel Hill, North Carolina, 1960). Clifford S. Griffin, *Their Brothers' Keepers; Moral Stewardship in the United States, 1800-1865* (New Brunswick, New Jersey, 1960) emphasizes the secular aspects of reform. Although it deals primarily with a somewhat later period, Timothy L. Smith, *Revivalism and Social Reform in Mid-Nineteenth-Century America* (New York, 1957), is a valuable aid to an understanding of the relation between religious ideas and the reform movements of the 1830's.

Of the vast literature on the antislavery movement, Dwight L. Dumond, *Antislavery Origins of the Civil War in the United States* (Ann Arbor, Michigan, 1939), and Gilbert H. Barnes, *The Antislavery Impulse 1830-1844* (New York, 1933), have special pertinence for an understanding of the western abolitionists. Russell B. Nye, *William Lloyd Garrison and the Humanitarian Reformers* (New York, 1955), provides a convenient, well-balanced summary. Antislavery activity in Illinois is traced, with some over-emphasis on the work of abolitionists from New York, in Hermann R. Muelder, *Fighters for Freedom, a History of Anti-Slavery Activities of Men and Women Associated with*

Knox College (New York, 1959). David Donald, *Lincoln Reconsidered* (New York, 1956), contains fresh views on the abolitionists; and in Donald W. Riddle, *The Martyrs, a Study in Social Control* (Chicago, 1931), one can see interesting parallels between the abolitionists and the early Christian martyrs.

A surprisingly large number of Lovejoy family papers have survived. The largest group is the Wickett-Wiswall Collection of Lovejoy Papers in the Southwest Collection of Texas Technological College, Lubbock. Other collections, which also yield important information about Elijah Lovejoy, his family, and his business affairs, are the Owen Lovejoy Papers in the William L. Clements Library of the University of Michigan, Ann Arbor; the Elijah P. Lovejoy Collection at Colby College, Waterville, Maine; and the Lovejoy Papers at the Illinois State Historical Library, Springfield. A small but revealing group of letters about his early career in Missouri is in the American Home Missionary Society Papers at the Chicago Theological Seminary. A few items concerning Lovejoy and his relation to the reform movement will be found at Illinois College, Jacksonville; the Chicago Historical Society; the Boston Public Library; the Library of Congress; and Monticello College, Godfrey, Illinois.

The main source for most of the public aspects of Lovejoy's life is the newspapers he edited throughout his career. Files of the interesting St. Louis *Times* are scattered and incomplete; the development of his ideas and the opposition to them may be traced in his St. Louis *Observer* and its successor, the Alton *Observer*. Other local newspapers, notably the St. Louis *Missouri Republican* and the Alton *Telegraph*, reflect contemporary public opinion, most of it hostile. The national antislavery press carried accounts of the stormy events of 1836 and 1837.

Because it contains correspondence that has otherwise disappeared, the most useful published source is Joseph C. Lovejoy and Owen Lovejoy, *Memoir of the Rev. Elijah P. Lovejoy; Who Was Murdered in Defense of the Liberty of the Press, at Alton, Illinois, Nov. 7, 1837* (New York, 1838). Of the many participants in the riot, only Edward Beecher published an account nearly contemporary with the event; his *Narrative of Riots at Alton: In Connection with the Death of Rev. Elijah P. Lovejoy* (Alton, 1838) is not only a keen analysis of the situation preceding the riots, but it is also probably the most eloquent defense of freedom of inquiry ever written in this country. William S. Lincoln, *Alton Trials: Of Winthrop S. Gilman, Who Was Indicted . . . for the Crime of Riot . . .* (New York, 1838), a compilation of the testimony during the trials of both those who destroyed the press and those who defended it, provides much information about the riots themselves. Four decades after the event, Henry Tanner, who as a young abolitionist had helped defend the press, published his reminiscences in *History of the Rise and Progress of the Alton Riots, Culminating in the Death of Rev. Elijah P. Lovejoy, November 7th, 1837* (Buffalo, New York, 1878). This appeared in greatly expanded form as *The Martyrdom of Lovejoy. An Account of the Life, Trials, and Perils of Elijah P. Lovejoy* (Chicago, 1881). Unfortunately when the opponents of Lovejoy wrote their memoirs, they largely ignored their participation in the events leading up to the riots.

Satisfactory secondary accounts of Lovejoy's career are few. The best short study is Frank H. Dugan, "An Illinois Martyrdom," Illinois State Historical Society, *Papers in Illinois History and Transactions,* 1938, pp. 111-157. John G. Gill's *Tide Without Turning; Elijah P. Lovejoy and Freedom of the Press* (Boston, 1958) is a colorful, semi-poetic account of Lovejoy's career, focusing on his defense of civil rights rather than on his role as an abolitionist. Hazel C. Wolf, *On Freedom's Altar: The Martyr Complex in the Abolition Movement* (Madison, Wisconsin, 1952) seeks to prove that Lovejoy and the other abolitionists she describes deliberately sought martyrdom. Numerous essays have been written and speeches made about Lovejoy as a defender of a free press. Interesting as many of these are for the interpretations they contain, they are largely theoretical and provide little biographical information.

Index